AN

HISTORICAL DISCOURSE

PRONOUNCED BEFORE THE

GRADUATES OF YALE COLLEGE,

August 14, 1850;

ONE HUNDRED AND FIFTY YEARS

AFTER THE

FOUNDING OF THAT INSTITUTION.

WITH AN

APPENDIX.

BY

THEODORE D. WOOLSEY,

PRESIDENT OF YALE COLLEGE.

NEW HAVEN:

PRINTED BY B. L. HAMLEN,

Printer to Yale College.

1850.

DISCOURSE.

THE occasion which assembles us together seems to prescribe what kind of discourse ought to be pronounced.* Nothing abstract or general, nothing drawn from the common stores of literature,—however well suited to other academical festivals, will meet the wishes or move the sympathies of the graduates of Yale College assembled at its third jubilee. Nor ought the present wants of the College or its projects of enlargement or fears of falling behind to occupy our thoughts at such a time. Our minds instinctively turn to *the College in the past*, to its history and its institutions from the beginning. We take greater pleasure, at a festival like this commemorative of the past, in tracing the stream down from its insignificant fountains to our present standing-place than in exploring or divining its further course. We resemble, far more than at our ordinary gatherings, a family collected from all quarters of the land to keep thanksgiving-day,—to render praises first to the God of families for his beneficent care, and then to revive the feeling of the family bond by recalling its old history and linking the present with the storied past. Am I not right,—respected graduates of our Alma Mater,—in supposing that a feeling like this of the family is in the minds of you all; that you have assembled with devout gratitude to the God of our fathers for having watched over this Seminary in its infancy, and enlarged it to its present degree of influence and usefulness;

* For an account of the proceedings at this celebration, see Appendix, No. I.

and that your thoughts, guided by a common feeling toward the College, of the nature of patriotism but warmer because less abstract, turn fondly back to its past fortunes as to those of a venerated ancestry. Let this then to which the occasion and your feelings invite, be my theme of discourse—the growth of the College, and the changes which it has undergone.

In the year 1752 the foundation of the College was noticed in an appropriate way,* but the series of collegiate years was erroneously counted from 1702 when the first degrees were given, instead of 1700 when the real foundation by donation of books took place. When, however, the complete century of the existence of Yale had revolved in 1800, no notice was taken of the event,—that being a time in the progress of our country, at which the present and the future filled the minds of men to the exclusion of the past. But now the minds of men in our country have leisure to study the past, and by means of that study national character, state feeling, and the attachment to institutions which have a historical basis are strengthened. It would have been then a gross violation of duty, a kind of indignity offered to our Alma Mater, whom we love, if the common voice of the graduates did not pronounce it necessary to honor this occasion. And it so happens that there is one peculiarity belonging to the present jubilee, in which no future one can participate:—the American revolution divides the history of the College almost exactly into two equal parts. From that great event our ancestors expected great results; and in particular certain young poets who had recently issued from these walls were kindled by it into prophecies of the world's regeneration which our example was to effect. But they were not aware of the alterations which the revolution was to bring about in life and manners, in

---

* See Appendix, No. II.

breaking up traditionary English usages, and giving almost a new structure to society. That such changes have followed in the train of the revolution the history of the College furnishes one of the most striking proofs. It is impossible indeed to separate the progress of a living and growing thing into two periods so distinct that causes shall not pass over from the one into the other, lingering even long after other causes peculiar to a new age shall have sprung up: yet, although many old usages, which have since become obsolete, stood their ground for a long time against the undermining power of this event, no one can hesitate to make it an era, and the most important era of our College history.

Standing therefore at a point as far distant on the one hand from this dividing line of the revolution, as the foundation of the College was on the other, let us cast our eyes over the progress of its affairs for eighty-five years until the beginning of Dr. Dwight's presidency,—after which time the memories of the living supersede the office of history;—and then upon that base-line measure its ancient institutions with a view of comparing them with the present.*

Sometime in the year 1700, ten ministers, acting by general consent for the ministry and the churches of the Colony of Connecticut, held a meeting at New Haven for the purpose of founding a Collegiate School; and this purpose they carried into effect at a subsequent meeting at Branford in the same year, when each person presented a number of books to the body, using words to this effect as he laid the books on the table: "I give these books for the founding of a College in this Colony." The next year in October a charter for the Collegiate School was granted by the legislature, and in November the Trustees, meeting at Saybrook,

* The part of the address which follows this paragraph and ends with the election of Rector Clap, was omitted in the delivery for want of time; and as was then stated to the audience a brief summary or table of contents was read in its place.

ordered "that there shall be and hereby is erected and formed a Collegiate School, wherein shall be taught the liberal arts and languages, in such place or places in Connecticut as the said Trustees with their associates and successors do or shall from time to time see cause to order." At the same time a resolution was passed, that for the best accommodation of all parts of Connecticut Colony with the neighboring Colony, the Collegiate School should be erected and formed at Saybrook, unless further considerations should offer themselves than the board had before them. In a subsequent meeting, however, held at New Haven, April 8th, 1702, the Trustees, retracing their steps a little, resolved that the place of the College should not be farther eastward than Saybrook, nor westward than New Haven. And in a meeting at Kennelworth (Killingworth,) in September of the same year, it was definitively ordered "that the Collegiate School be settled in the town of Saybrook, but be continued at Kennelworth [where the Rector, Mr. Pierson, was settled,] till Providence shall enable the Trustees to fix the same in said Saybrook."

The College thus created and placed at Saybrook was called into existence at a time when the number of inhabitants in the Colony did not amount to twenty thousand, and when a considerable part of the territory of the colony was a wilderness.* Now as there was a College not very far distant to which the inhabitants of the colony had looked as the place of higher education for their sons, and to the support of which they had contributed, it has been asked why the step was taken of founding another College in a less wealthy and a smaller community. A solution of this problem has been found in the existence of a disaffected theological party, who being deprived of influence at Harvard, and communicating their jealousies to some of the Con-

---

* See Appendix, No. III.

necticut ministers, urged the establishment of a new Seminary where the strict faith of the Puritans might find a refuge. But such a ground for the new Seminary has been shown to be, as far as Connecticut is concerned, a mere theory and will probably not be received for historical truth. There is no cause for believing that any dissatisfaction with Harvard, or any want of confidence in its government existed in the body of Connecticut ministers and churches whom the original Trustees of this College represented. The projectors of the new Seminary indeed received counsel as to their charter from gentlemen in Massachusetts in civil life, who may have belonged to a party dissatisfied with the leading influence at Harvard, but they adopted the suggestions of these gentlemen in no important particular, and probably had every thing arranged and determined upon before the advice was communicated.* The true reason for founding a new College lay much more on the surface of things than this which has been assigned. It was, to cite the words of a manuscript written soon afterwards, "the want of learning and learned men both in church and state, and the great difficulty and extreme charges of educating children at Harvard College in Cambridge," that induced "several worthy gentlemen of this Colony of Connecticut" "to prefer a petition before the general assembly of this Colony for license to erect a Collegiate School." If we take into account the length of time which was consumed on a journey on horseback to Cambridge, the positive cost of the journey, the difficulty of communication with a child placed there, together with the poverty of Connecticut which long impeded the growth and had nearly starved the infancy of Yale College, it will not be strange if parents hesitated long before they sent their children to a place so remote, and

* See Appendix, No. IV, and consult Prof. Kingsley's review of President Quincy's history of Harvard University, in the Biblical Repository for July and October, 1841, and January, 1842.

wished for a cheaper place of education within the bounds of their own Colony. Nor was a College here a new thought: on the contrary, long before the expiration of the seventeenth century such a thing was talked of, and movements were made to effect it, especially in the settlements on the coast and within the limits of the colony of New Haven.*

The charter and plan of this College differed considerably from the model which had before been followed. A College, in the modern sense of that word, was an institution which arose within a university, probably within that of Paris or of Oxford first, being intended either as a kind of boarding school, or for the support of scholars destitute of means, who were here to live under particular supervision. By degrees it became more and more the custom that teachers should be attached to these establishments. And as they grew in favor they were resorted to by persons of means who paid for their board; and this to such a degree, that at one time the colleges included nearly all the members of the University of Paris. In the English universities the colleges may have been first established by a master who gathered pupils around him, for whose board and instruction he provided. He exercised them perhaps in logic and the other liberal arts, and repeated the university lectures as well as superintended their morals. As his scholars grew in number, he associated with himself other teachers, who thus acquired the name of *fellows*. Thus it naturally happened that the government of colleges, even of those which were founded by the benevolence of pious persons, was in the hands of a principal called by various names, such as rector, president, provost or master, and of fellows, all of whom were resident within the walls of the same edifices where the students lived. When charitable munificence

---

* See Appendix, No. V.

went so far as to provide for the support of a greater number of Fellows than were needed, some of them were entrusted, as tutors, with the instruction of the undergraduates, while others performed various services within their college or passed a life of learned leisure.* Such was the system in England after which Harvard College was originally modelled. Under a board of overseers answering to the visiters in English Colleges, were placed a President, five Fellows, and a Bursar, who were to reside at the College and to be charged with its government and management. When Increase Mather acted as President without leaving his church in Boston, it was entirely consistent with the original plan that the vote was passed requiring his residence at Cambridge, which led to his resignation. In the course of time, but not until after the foundation of this College, the Board of President and Fellows there came to exercise government without instruction, and the Fellows ceased to be resident; the result of which was the existence of two boards instead of one, controlling the officers of the institution.

The plan of the new College in Connecticut, differed from that of its elder sister at Harvard, in not providing for a body of resident Fellows. The founders of the latter coming fresh from Oxford and Cambridge, could not conceive of a college without officers of this name. But between 1636 and 1700 the old recollections had passed away, so that in our earliest charter only a "rector or master, tutors, an usher or other officers" are spoken of, as if a school rather than a college lay in the minds of the founders; with which also the modest title of Collegiate School well accords. The charter of 1745 first speaks of the President and Fellows. But the latter are so called by a misnomer, which

* See Savigny Geschichte des Röm. rechts im Mittelalter, 3, § 131, and Huber's English Universities, translated by Newman. Huber distinguishes between halls and colleges, 1, § 28, § 104.

perhaps the usage of non-residence, then nearly established at Harvard, will serve to explain. Thus the Fellows stood in the relation of overseers; holding the same connection with the College, which is implied in the titles of trustees, undertakers or partners, which the first charter gave them. The Rector was originally, but not necessarily one of their number. And such continued to be the state of things until after the deposition in 1722 of Rector Cutler, who had not been elected into the board of trustees, although there was a vacancy when he was appointed to his office. In the ensuing year, however, an act " in explanation of and in addition to" the original charter made the Rector by virtue of his office one of the Trustees, and the new charter of 1745 contains the same provision. It is worthy of remark that although the Rector had this official prerogative, Rector Williams, who entered upon his office in 1726, did not take his seat among the Trustees until 1728; the reason of which appears to have been, that the board of Trustees was already full, and that thus the act of 1723, which was not intended to be in conflict with the original charter or to alter it, could not go into effect. In the year named, one of the Trustees having died, the Rector claimed and by express vote was admitted to his seat.

It may not be amiss here to call the notice of my hearers to two circumstances, in the constitution of the governing body of this College, for which we have not a little reason to be thankful. The first is the homogeneousness of the Trustees at the beginning. Selected by the ministers and churches of Connecticut, at a time when all were of one way of thinking as to dogmas and ecclesiastical order, they were in fact representatives of the colony, and carried with them the confidence of all intelligent persons. Had division of sentiments or of counsels prevailed at the first, it is not easy to see how the College could have existed at all, or have been cherished if founded. And at that time it was certainly better, considering the circumstances of the colony, that the Trustees should be ministers exclusively. But in the age of the revolutionary war a new state of things had matured. A large number of laymen of education had grown up, who were competent to see the great importance of the College to the State. Religious sects also had separated from the original stock of Congregationalism, who would be tempted to look with a jealous eye upon the College, and who might harm it seriously, if it should not enjoy the good will of the State government. And the State having now become a sovereignty, instead of a colonial dependant upon the mother country, might be tempted to use that sovereignty without control, to the detriment of chartered institutions, if it were not propitiated by having a share in their management. To this altered state of things the alteration in the Charter corresponded, which in 1792 introduced members of the State government into the Board of Fellows. The connection thus formed with the State has proved, as we shall see, a fortunate thing for the College. And it is a pity that the parties to this transaction could not have united in a similar arrangement a quarter of a century before.

Another fortunate circumstance in the constitution of the College was, that the early acts of the men who became the first Trustees under the charter, made it certain that they and no other body were the founders. The act of founding consisted in their giving forty folios for the purpose of estabing a College in the Colony. This question of who the founders were, came up in 1763 near the close of President Clap's administration, when nine individuals in a memorial to the General Assembly represented, that the assembly,—inasmuch as the charter emanated from them, and they had given a donation of money to the Trustees with the charter,—were the founders of the College, and as such had a right to appoint visitors; which act they prayed the assembly to perform, and to authorize an appeal from sentences of the College

Faculty and Corporation, to the Governor and Council. They prayed likewise that the assembly would issue a committee of visitation, and alleged that such an appeal and visitation were necessary to preserve good order and orthodoxy in religion.

President Clap in his history of the College, published three years afterwards, has given us his line of defence in his reply, which has drawn forth high commendation from a great jurist graduated at this College,* and was founded on the same principles and supported by some of the same law authorities, upon which the great case of Dartmouth College was defended by its eminent counsel and graduate, Mr. Webster. He shows that the ten ministers who met at Branford in 1700, being a society and a quasi-corporation by nomination and consent of a body of ministers and people, and having made a donation to the College as well as received property in trust for it before the charter, were in reality its founders by the common law, and thus had the right of visitation which they transmitted to their legal successors. He says that gratitude indeed was due to the Legislature as the greatest benefactors of the College, and that they had the same power over it as over other persons and estates in the commonwealth, but that this did not imply visitatorial power, and indeed the charter of 1745 had expressly called the first Trustees founders of the College. In regard to the argument that visitors were needed to preserve the orthodoxy of the College, he stated that all the means were taken to preserve orthodoxy in the College which human prudence could devise, and there was no certainty that visitors appointed by the civil order would be equally orthodox. There was but one person who was sworn to maintain orthodoxy, and that was the king's most excellent majesty,

* See Chancellor Kent's Address before the Graduates, delivered in 1831, p. 30.

who took oath at his coronation to maintain and preserve the true protestant religion with the worship, and discipline of the church of Scotland, which is built upon the Westminster confession of faith. By this reference to the king, he perhaps intended to throw out a threat that, if the subject was pushed to an extreme, he would carry an appeal across the water, which of all things would have been most dreaded and disliked. Whether his reasoning or apprehension of the result prevailed, the subject was not pushed farther.

There was one mistake, as experience proved, in the first proceedings of the Trustees; and that was the establishment of the College at Saybrook. That they hesitated before deciding to do this and perhaps were divided in their own minds, appears from some of their earliest resolutions which I have already cited. Nor is it a matter of much question why they determined in favor of Saybrook. Of the ten Trustees, seven belonged to towns upon the seaside; —Stonington and Fairfield being the extreme points represented. Saybrook lay not far from the middle point of the coast; and had the advantage of being the spot where the line of towns on the river, which principally skirted the western bank, met the line of maritime settlements. Much of the higher country, and especially almost all the present county of Litchfield,—which afterwards sent to the College so many scholars of vigorous minds,—was as yet unreclaimed wilderness. Thus Saybrook was a convenient point, where two streams of population met. But after the establishment of the College there, the inconveniences, arising from the sparseness of the settlement, together with other embarrassments naturally pressing upon a new institution in a small and poor colony, had nearly crushed the College in its infancy. The first Rector, Mr. Pierson, who lived in the next town to Saybrook, never removed to that place, because the funds did not allow the erection of a building for his accommodation, and for this reason the students were kept at Killingworth until his death in 1707. After this, another of the Trustees, living so far off as Milford, discharged the duties of a Rector, as well as he could without removing his residence. The Senior Class was with him at Milford, while the other Classes resided at Saybrook under the instruction of the tutors. The students lived scattered about in the town, some of them a mile from the place of instruction. Complaints arose among them against these instructors on the score of youth and inexperience; and sundry of them, says President Clap, "who lived near Hartford and Wethersfield, said that it was a hardship for them to be obliged to reside at Saybrook, when they could as well or better be instructed nearer home." These complaints, as appears from what subsequently occurred, were either suggested to the students with a design to help forward a removal of the College, or else made a removal, which for other reasons was projected, seem still more desirable. In this state of affairs, the Trustees met at Saybrook in April, 1716, and although they found the causes of complaint against the Tutors not such as to call for any new arrangements, yet they allowed the students to place themselves under other instructors until the next Commencement. The small band of undergraduates,—who would altogether not amount to much more than a quarter of one of the present classes,—were thus scattered: the larger part were collected again at Wethersfield under the tuition of Elisha Williams, afterwards Rector; while the few who remained at Saybrook were driven thence by the small pox in the course of the summer to East Guilford.

The Trustees left Saybrook after the meeting in April just mentioned, with no other thought, so far as we can learn, than that they were to make the best they could of the College in its actual location. It was therefore a matter of profound surprise to the greater part of the body, when, not long afterward they learned that two of their number had laid a petition before the legislature at its spring session in Hartford, having reference to the affairs of the College.* This petition, after representing the languishing state of the institution arising mainly from want of funds, goes on to say that the people of Hartford had in conjunction with other well-minded persons, subscribed such a sum of money as might put the school into a flourishing condition. They then offer the request,—which is to be considered as the condition of the subscriptions,—that the College may be fixed at Hartford, and suggest some reasons why it should be. The reasons are that Hartford was more in the centre of the Colony, and was surrounded with many considerable towns, upon which account it might be supposed that the number of students would be greater than if it were at any other place, which had not the like situation. They add also that several persons† in the neighboring province had assured them, not only that they would contribute toward the settling of the school there, but also that they would send their youth thither for education. There had already been subscribed, they say, a sum of between six and seven hundred pounds for this purpose, which, they had good reasons to suppose that other donations would swell to the sum of a thousand pounds or upwards.

It is pretty evident from the tenor of this petition, that the Trustees in their meeting at Saybrook in the month of April, although they had adjourned without taking any measures to remove the College, had talked over the possibility of such an act, and that the petitioning Trustees who were the two ministers of Hartford, were well aware that the majority of the board would not transplant the College from the seaside. Had they contemplated in their

---

* See Appendix, No. VI.

† Perhaps in the towns on Connecticut river belonging to the Massachusetts Colony.

petition the step of effecting the removal by act of the legislature, it would have been highly irregular, and have involved a violation of the charter, which as we have already seen, allowed the Trustees to establish the College in such convenient place or places as to them should seem meet. It is however pretty certain that they contemplated no such unlawful interference of the legislature, but only sought for such an expression of opinion and perhaps such pecuniary inducements, as would have more weight with the Trustees than any apprehension could have, that their chartered rights would be invaded.

The petitioners to the legislature in speaking of the Hartford subscription, mention that in several other places it had been proposed to do the same thing. What places are intended it does not certainly appear unless that Wethersfield was one of them. New Haven and Saybrook would be likely to be of the number, but unless Mr. Johnson in his account of this affair is misinformed, the subscriptions there did not begin to circulate until sometime in the summer after the Hartford movement. Meanwhile the legislature had called the Trustees before them to show them "their difficulties and what might be by them thought expedient to be done therein, in order to the proceedings of [the] assembly for the better advancement of the Collegiate School." Some of the Trustees obeyed the call, and persuaded the legislature not to take the petition into consideration, until the autumnal meeting at New Haven. They also agreed among themselves that, unless they could unanimously decide at the next Commencement where the College should be established, they would desire the assembly to nominate a place for it. At Commencement in September, one of the two Tutors resigned,—the other having left his office in the summer,—and the institution was reduced to its lowest point of depression: it had no regular instructor, a rector pro tempore, and about twenty-five scholars dispersed through the colony.

At this time also an attempt was made to unite the minds of the Trustees upon Saybrook without success. But now a new difficulty arose. Several of the Trustees who had not appeared before the legislature in May, refused to accede to the agreement of the rest, that the affair should be referred to the legislature if they could not agree among themselves, and declared that this act was illegal; as it undoubtedly was, no legal warning of a meeting having been issued. The whole Board, with the exception of the two Hartford ministers, came at a meeting held during the session of the legislature in October at New Haven to this same conclusion, that their meeting at Hartford was illegal and not binding, and that it was inexpedient to address the general court. They were moreover advised by the upper house or council by no means to address the lower house; by which we are to understand that it was apprehended, that the majority of the lower house might favor the Hartford petitioners. Having thus set aside the agreement made at Hartford to put the affairs of the College into the hands of the legislature,—an agreement not certainly binding in law, but binding in honor and conscience upon those who were parties to it,—they decided to use the powers which the charter had given them, resolving first to remove the school from Saybrook, to which all agreed except the Trustee from Lyme on the other side of the river; and then to transplant it to New Haven, in which vote five out of eight who were present concurred, while of the three who dissented, one, the Trustee from Lyme, was of opinion that, if removed from that place, it could go nowhere more fitly than to New Haven. Of the two absent Trustees one was bed-ridden, another was known to be in favor of New Haven. It is quite probable that the majority of the Trustees, in this decisive and important measure, acted in concert with the principal magistrates of the Colony and the members of the Council, and went forward through their subsequent embarrassments assured of support in that quarter.

Having thus determined where the College should be placed, the Trustees at this time, or not long after, resolved to commence a college building, and applied to Governor Saltonstall for a plan of it. They also appointed two new Tutors, of whom only one repaired to New Haven. The Senior Class was there instructed by Mr. Noyes, the minister of the town, but nearly half of the students persisted in remaining at Wethersfield, and two staid at Saybrook. The important measure of removing the College to New Haven was re-enacted by a vote of six Trustees in April, 1717. In May of the same year the two dissatisfied Trustees presented a memorial to the legislature, complaining that the majority of the Board had violated their word in refusing to ask the assembly to nominate a place for the College, and alleging also that the vote of removal to New Haven was not in accordance with the charter, because one of the five Trustees who were in it was not legally qualified; and that thus, as the whole number was ten, there was no majority. Probably, at the same session, a remonstrance against the selection of New Haven to be the seat of the College was laid before the General Assembly, from sundry inhabitants of Hartford and New London Counties, urging that the interests of those,* the larger counties, had not been consulted in this act of the Trustees of the College. In consequence of these memorials a resolution was passed in the lower house, but rejected in the upper, requiring the Trustees to give their attendance at the assembly as speedily as might be, and to lay before that body the circumstances of the Collegiate School.

From this time until October, 1717, when the assembly met at New Haven, extreme dissatisfaction was felt by a part of the colony with the result to which the Trustees had come. At Commencement they re-affirmed their proceed-

---

* Comp. Appendix, No. III.

ings, and strove to remove all color of illegality from their former acts. One more attempt, and, as it proved, the last, was made during the session of the legislature that autumn to reverse the proceedings of the Trustees, and to fix upon a new place for the College. The lower house, in something of a passion, voted that "the Trustees be desired and directed to come as speedily as might be to this assembly to show the reasons of the late proceedings, and particularly why they or any of them had ordered a collegiate school to be built at New Haven without the allowance or knowledge of [the] assembly." This strong vote, which might imply a disposition to lay violent hands upon the charter, was so far modified in the upper house, that the Trustees were simply desired to appear before the legislature. They came accordingly, and after fruitless attempts to arrive at some agreement among themselves, drew up a memorial containing their answer to objections against New Haven as well as against the validity of their proceedings. Meanwhile the two houses of the legislature were as discordant with one another as the two parties among the Trustees. The lower house, as if the whole matter were still open and fell within their jurisdiction, put to vote the claims of different places to receive the College. Saybrook had but six votes out of between sixty and seventy. The house also divided between Middletown and New Haven, with a result of thirty-five votes in favor of the former and thirty-two in favor of the latter. The upper house, on the other hand, planted itself upon the ground that the Trustees had a right to decide where the College should be; that they had so decided in a legal meeting; and that all objections against the validity of their proceedings were frivolous. After some time it was agreed that the Trustees should appear before the houses assembled in joint session, and make known the grounds which both sides had for their proceedings. Mr. Davenport of Stamford, in the name of the majority, vindicated them from all charges of irregularity, and set forth the factious management of the other side; while one of the dissatisfied Trustees urged the point that the vote of the Board was not legal, inasmuch as a legal majority did not concur in it. The upper house, says a contemporary manuscript, "all as one man agreed that they would advise the Trustees settling the school at New Haven to go on with it, esteeming their cause just and good; and they sent it down to the lower house where there [were] great throes and pangs and controversy and mighty struggling: at length they put it to vote, and there were six more for the side of New Haven than the contrary; and thus, at length, the up river party had their will in having the school settled by the General Court, though sorely against their will, at New Haven; but many owned themselves fairly beat."

Of the vote which is mentioned in this extract we have found no other record. Its passage, probably, was a prelude to another resolution which, so far as the legislature was concerned, is to be regarded as a final adjustment of the whole affair. This resolution, as first passed in the upper house, ran as follows: "Whereas it has been esteemed by some a considerable hardship upon the counties of Hartford and New London that a house for the Collegiate School has been built at New Haven, at such a distance from these counties and particularly, (as is alleged,) to the town of Hartford, which was anciently the seat of the principal administration of power in the colony, therefore for the peace and better regulation and balance of public benefit of affairs in the colony, and forasmuch as it will in all probability conduce very much to the good order and honor of our public administration to have a fair and suitable building of our courts of election in Hartford and for other public occasions,

Be it therefore enacted, &c. "That ten miles square of land in quantity in one entire piece shall be sold for the procuring of one thousand pounds, and for the encouragement of purchasers it is hereby ordered that the same be erected into a manor, and that the purchasers thereof shall have all the privileges of a township annexed thereunto. And it is further enacted, that £800 of the said thousand shall be applied to the erecting of a fitting house for holding of the assembly and other courts in Hartford in such form as this court shall direct. And that £200 of the said thousand be given to the Trustees of the Collegiate School for carrying on and finishing the house erected for said school in New Haven."*

This bill, with the exception of the provision that the land to be sold should be erected into a manor, passed the lower house also, and thus peace was restored to the legislature and to most parts of the Colony. It took a long time, however, for the dissentient Trustees to come into the measures of the majority, as the legislature had done; nor were the people of Saybrook disposed to give up the library, yet remaining there, without a struggle. I will dwell on the lingering opposition no longer than to say, that a portion of the students were retained at Wethersfield through the year 1718, by the influence of the disaffected Trustees; that a Commencement was held there in the autumn of that year, and that although the General Court in October, 1718, ordered the students to repair to New Haven, they rendered only a formal obedience to this mandate, and strove to injure the government of the College and to throw its affairs into confusion. At length the conciliatory measures of the majority of the Trustees, united to the obvious fact that the College had a permanent footing at New Haven, overcame all opposition. Some of those who had shown the most active and even factious opposition to the measures which prevailed, returned to kindliness of feeling and became again friends of the College. In process of time one who had been the principal instrument in the rival project at Wethersfield was

* Johnson assigns this act to October, 1718, instead of 1717. Copies of the State Records, which lie before me, assign it to 1717.

appointed to the rectorate of the College at New Haven, and earnestly promoted its interests.

The excited feelings of the people of Saybrook were shown in violently resisting the attempts to convey the library to New Haven,—a resistance carried so far that the door of the house where it was kept had to be broken in, and the civil force of the county to be called out for the protection of the books, while the wagons for transporting the books were invaded by night, many of the books carried away, and some of the bridges torn down upon the road to New Haven. About two hundred and sixty volumes were wanting, when the rest, above a thousand in number, were put up in the library of the new collegiate building.*

If now we revert to the motives by which the major part of the Trustees were actuated, in their persevering and successful determination to transplant the College to New Haven, we shall find them to be partly sectional, and partly of a more enlightened character. That a sectional feeling of the seaside against the river and the interior somewhat entered into the affair, is made probable by the fact that, as we have before seen, seven out of ten of the Trustees belonged to this part of the Colony, and that Mr. Johnson in his narrative constantly sets the seaside and the "up-river" Trustees against one another. The reasons which they allege for preferring New Haven, in their memorial to the legislature of October 22d, 1717, are the "conveniency of its situation, agreeableness of the air and soil, the probability of providing what will be necessary for the convenience of the scholars, as cheap or cheaper than at other places, together with many other weighty considerations to us satisfying; whereunto may be added the largest sums of money by far subscribed by particular gentlemen for building an house for the school in said town." Among the "weighty considerations" which in-

* For the authorities followed in this account of the removal of the College, see Appendix, No. VI.

fluenced them, is to be included that the situation was more convenient and accessible for the western colonies than any of its rivals.* That they took this into account was certainly evidence of enlightened policy, and their judgment was justified by the fact, that until Nassau Hall and Columbia Colleges provided for the wants of New Jersey and New York, those colonies looked principally for their supply of educated men to this institution, and sent their sons here to be educated. And again, as it respects convenience of situation, it would seem that no inconsiderable part of the stream of travel from the eastern to the western colonies, instead of going over the height of land to Connecticut river, passed down from eastern Massachusetts to New London and thence pursued the line of the coast to New Haven, where it united with the other portion from Connecticut river. The accessibleness of this place has doubtless contributed to the success of the College ; and it remains to be seen how far this advantage will be diminished in the future by the newest mode of communication, which brings almost all institutions of learning within convenient reach.

The College had thus, from being almost an airy nothing, received a local habitation, and was also, in the course of the year 1718, destined to have that name given to its newly commenced building, by which, since the charter of 1745, the whole institution has been designated. The reasons for adopting the name of Yale College, after a liberal benefactor in England who was descended from one of the original settlers of New Haven, are too well known to require us to dwell upon them. It may not, however, be uninteresting to read here an extract relating to this subject from the manuscript, written at the time by one of the college officers, to which we have already several times referred. "The building went forward apace, so that the hall and library were finished by Commencement. A few days before Commence-

---

* See Appendix, No. VI.

ment, came the news of the good success of some gentlemen's endeavors to procure some donations from Great Britain. For at Boston arrived a large box of books, the picture and arms of King George, and two hundred pounds sterling worth of English goods, all to the value of eight hundred pounds in our money, from Governor Yale of London, which greatly revived our hearts and disheartened our opposers.—[We were] favored and honored with the presence of his honor, Governor Saltonstall, and his lady, and the Hon. Col. Taylor of Boston, and the Lieutenant Governor and the whole Superior Court, at our Commencement, September 10th, 1718, where the Trustees present,—those gentlemen being present,—in the hall of our new College, first most solemnly named our College by the name of Yale College, to perpetuate the memory of the honorable Gov. Elihu Yale, Esq., of London, who had granted so liberal and bountiful a donation for the perfecting and adorning of it. Upon which the honorable Col. Taylor represented Governor Yale in a speech expressing his great satisfaction; which ended, we passed to the Church and there the Commencement was carried on. In which affair, in the first place, after prayer an oration was had by the saluting orator, James Pierpont, and then the disputations as usual; which concluded, the Rev. Mr. Davenport [one of the Trustees and minister of Stamford] offered an excellent oration in Latin, expressing their thanks to Almighty God and Mr. Yale under him for so public a favor and so great regard to our languishing school. After which were graduated ten young men, whereupon the Hon. Gov. Saltonstall, in a Latin speech, congratulated the Trustees in their success and in the comfortable appearance of things with relation to their school. All which ended, the gentlemen returned to the College Hall, where they were entertained with a splendid dinner, and the ladies, at the same time, were also entertained in the Library; after which they sung the four first verses in the 63d Psalm, and so the day ended."*

My hearers will not fail to have remarked that the ladies were put upon an intellectual diet, while the gentlemen had access to the good things which the hall afforded. Probably complaints would have come down to posterity, if the treatment of the two sexes had been reversed.

Scarcely had the College emerged from the waves of discord and reached a secure port, when it was exposed to another trial. In 1719 a new Rector was chosen, the Rev. Timothy Cutler, then minister of Stratford, and a graduate of Harvard.† He removed to New Haven, and had filled his office for something more than three years, when he declared his conviction that the Anglican theory of church government was the true one, and the orders of the New England ministry invalid. The only Tutor, Mr. Daniel Brown, shared his opinions; and several neighboring ministers, most of whom were graduates of the College, and several had been officers, were more or less of the same way of thinking. That these gentlemen were honest in their persuasion seems undoubted; and, indeed, under the circumstances in which they found themselves, the first champions of an unwelcome theory in the Colony, and dissenters from the church order there established, there was every motive for dishonest or timid men to conceal their opinions. There seems to be little doubt that they studied together the points of difference between the church of England and other sects which had separated from it, and that books in the library of the College wrought this change in their sentiments. A

* See Appendix, No. VII.

† In 1718, before this choice was made, it was voted "that the Rev. Mr. Andrew do write, according to his discretion, to Mr. Henry Flynt, to obtain of him some good encouragement that he will accept the office of a Rector's post in our Yale College, our eyes being upon him for Rector." Mr. Flynt declined, preferring the office of Fellow and Tutor at Harvard, which he filled for many years afterward.

departure for the first time in the Colony, and of so many at once, from the views of the New England churches, and a return to that church from which the pilgrims had fled into the wilderness, filled the minds of men with apprehension and gloom,—feelings which extended into the neighboring Colony. I suppose that greater alarm would scarcely be awakened now, if the Theological Faculty of the College were to declare for the Church of Rome, avow their belief in transubstantiation, and pray to the Virgin Mary. A public disputation was held at the Commencement of 1722, in which Gov. Saltonstall, who had been a minister, took part against the Anglican doctrine; and the result was, that two of the gentlemen who had united with the Rector in his views, professed themselves convinced that their ministerial ordination was valid, while the Rector, persisting in his opinions, was excused by the Trustees from further service.* The Tutor also resigned his post at the same time. This act of deposition all will allow to have been necessary in a seminary, which was intended for the training of ministers, as much as for any other purpose; and which was founded endowed and governed by adherents of the Congregational system. It was followed by an act of the Trustees imposing a test, the aim of which was to maintain in their soundness the faith and church theory of the Puritans.

It may not be impertinent to add that these gentlemen, who thus left the Puritan platform, were not inclined to array themselves in hostility to the College. They were rather inclined to regard it as a hopeful place, where, in process of time, views similar to their own would flourish. In particular, one of them, Mr. afterwards Dr. Johnson, first President of Columbia College, appears to have taken a friendly interest in the welfare of the College, and to have rendered to it important services. Subsequently a large number of the more eminent and active Episcopal ministers, both in New

---

* See Appendix, No. VIII.

England and to the westward of it, were educated at Yale College.*

The four next years were passed in fruitless attempts to induce some one to accept the Rectorate.† This subject occupied the attention not only of the Trustees but also of the legislature, for in 1724 we find that "a gracious message" was received by the Trustees assembled in Hartford from the honorable, the legislature, by the gentlemen deputed from both houses, expressing their great desire that an able Rector of Yale College may be provided and settled there as soon as may be. To which the Trustees, after returning their hearty thanks for the generous concern of the legislature for the welfare of the school in this and former instances, reply that they had "chosen the Rev. Mr. Wigglesworth, Professor of Divinity at Cambridge, to be the Rector; and in case of a disappointment, the Rev. William Russell of Middletown; and if he also should decline, the Rev. Elisha Williams of Newington." Before this, as we learn from College documents, Mr. Nathaniel Williams, of Boston, was applied to without success to fill the same office.‡ At length, in 1726, the Rev. Elisha Williams, whom we have already had occasion to mention, was appointed to the Rectorate, and, having accepted the office the next year, continued to discharge its duties until 1739, when he retired on the ground of impaired health. His Rectorate seems to have been, on the whole, a time of growth and of success for the College.§ The most important event of its history, during these years, was Berkeley's donation of a farm at Newport, and of a large number of valuable books amounting in all to about a thousand, of which eight hundred and fifty were given at one time in the year 1734.

---

* Such as Drs. Caner, Chandler, Leaming, Seabury, Beach and Jarvis.

† See Appendix, No. IX.

‡ His letter declining the place, and giving the unwillingness of his wife and family to change their residence as the cause, is dated Boston, May 13, 1723.

§ See Appendix, No. X.

On the resignation of Rector Williams, the Rev. Thomas Clap, minister of Windham in Connecticut, was chosen his successor, and held the office for twenty-seven years, until 1766. He was a man surpassed by no one who has since taken his place, in vigor of mind energy and determination. His scientific studies lay especially in the department of mathematical science, in which, for that day, and for this country as then situated, he was no mean proficient; and studies of that description appear to have thriven under his fostering care, far more than they had done before. Soon after he entered upon his office began the religious awakening in New England, which was followed by irregularities and fanaticism, which many of its most zealous promoters greatly deplored. In endeavoring to repress these irregularities in the College, President Clap, with the Fellows, committed the error, in the case of David Brainerd, of punishing opinions casually dropped, as though they proceeded from a malignant intention; and in another case, the error of persecuting, by College power, dissenters from the legally established church order.* At a later day, when theological opinion had somewhat changed, he felt alarmed, lest the old landmarks should be removed, which the fathers had set up. He therefore strove to guard the College from the intrusion of what he conceived to be error by making it a separate religious society, and by subjecting its Fellows and instructors to a more rigorous test. This circumstance, together with a certain inflexibility of purpose, and a rigor in administration, which perhaps a change of the moral and social tone of the country after the war of 1756 rendered the less welcome, exposed him to much obloquy without the College from a party who seem to have industriously fomented disorders within its walls. Certain it is that in the last years of his Presidency, while the College charter was attacked and the press was issuing pamphlets against his administra-

* See Appendix, No. XI.

tion, more than usual lawlessness prevailed among the students, so that perhaps the College never presented a more disorganized state; for which, according to the traditions which old graduates have retained, a body of somewhat inefficient Tutors was partly responsible. He resigned his office in July, 1766, and died the January following. In his farewell oration in Latin, delivered at the Commencement of that year, he says: "Hujusce Collegii status semper ita se habuit ut pluribus curis negotiis ac laboribus implicatus fui quam uni homini competeret, vel aliis præfectis usitatum fuit. Quas quidem curas et labores ad hujusce Collegii emolumentum per annos viginti fere septem alacritate maxima et oblectatione summa peregi. Sed nunc ætate provectus ac laboribus fatigatus ideoque vitæ privatæ et solitudinis deliciarum avidissimus, officium meum libentissime resigno. Satis diu vitam egi publicam. Sat habui honoris, plus nimio oneris: cum studio et conatu ardentissimo [labores meos contuli] ad hujusce societatis decus et emolumentum maximum promovendum, præsertim ut religionis puræ principiis juvenum mentes imbuantur." What he here says of himself is most strictly true. Probably no College officer in New England has ever devoted himself to his College with more untiring zeal and disinterestedness, and, on the whole, with more success than President Clap.*

President Clap's administration was marked by a gradual growth and improvement in the College. Its number of students amounted, at the close of his office, to one hundred and seventy. New buildings were erected which still subsist. Some additions were made to the permanent funds. The laws were remodelled. The charter was amended and improved. But the most characteristic measure of this period was the appointment of a Professor of Theology, and the establishment of a separate religious society and church in the College. This measure, which was dictated as well by doctrinal alarms on

* See Appendix, No. XII.

the President's part, as by the conviction that a College, being a community wholly unlike others in which it is placed, needs a different sort of religious instruction, was warmly opposed even by some members of the Corporation, who affected to see in it an attack upon the parity and established order of the churches in the Colony. They went so far as to carry up a memorial to the legislature, which, however, met with no success. The measure which they opposed has proved a wise one, and has been since sanctioned by the voice of other Colleges. Nor can we doubt, although there are peculiarities of a delicate nature attending a religious society in an academical body, that the good to be gained can be secured in no other way as effectually.

I have already had occasion to say that a cloud came over the latter years of President Clap's collegiate life in consequence of enmity to the government of the College without its walls and insubordination within. In 1761 a memorial was presented to the General Assembly by three citizens of the Colony, representing the great disorders at the College, the arbitrary powers with which the Faculty were clothed in order to suppress them, and the dislike felt by the students to their governors; and praying that the assembly would exercise a visitor's powers in searching into these grievances. No action was taken upon this memorial, but another of kindred spirit, presented two years after, gave occasion to President Clap's argument before the legislature to which I have referred in an earlier part of this discourse.

On the resignation of President Clap, after an ineffectual attempt to induce the Rev. James Lockwood to accept the Presidency, the Corporation contented themselves with investing the Professor of Divinity, the Rev. Dr. Daggett, with presidential authority for the time. This interregal relation to the College he occupied for eleven years, until 1777, when he resigned these functions, but retained those of the professorship of divinity until his death in 1780. He was a respectable preacher, but not a man of any uncommon abilities or learning.* He was ably supported by a body of superior men in the Tutorial office, among whom we find the names of Ebenezer Baldwin, Judge Mitchell, Judge Trumbull, Drs. Strong, Buckminster and Dwight. No important changes in the arrangements of the College at this time deserve to be mentioned, unless it be the establishment of a professorship of mathematics and natural philosophy, and the temporary introduction of some new studies.

About the time of President Daggett's resignation, and while Dr. Stiles was deliberating on the offer of the presidency made to him, the trials attending the revolutionary war pressed most heavily upon the welfare of the College. We find the following resolution on record, under date of April 1st, 1777. "Whereas the difficulties of subsisting the students in this town are so great, the price of provisions and board so high, and the avocations from study, occasioned by the state of public affairs, so many,—difficulties which still increase, and render it very inconvenient for the students to reside here at present, and yet considering the great importance that they be under the best advantages of instruction and learning circumstances will permit,—voted that, in the opinion of this Board, it is necessary to provide some other convenient place or places where the classes may reside under their respective Tutors, until God, in his kind providence, shall open a door for their return to this fixed and ancient seat of learning." By other resolutions provision was made for the removal of the library and papers, as well as for the security of the College buildings during the temporary absence of the students, with the view, especially, of preventing troops from being quartered in them, unless absolute necessity should require it. In conformity with these votes the Freshman Class was removed to Farmington, the Junior and Sophomore to Glastenbury, and Mr. afterwards

---

* See Appendix, No. XIII.

President Dwight, then Tutor, was requested to provide a suitable place for the Seniors, and to busy himself with their instruction during the short remainder of their academical life. The Professor of Mathematics was ordered to reside with the two middle classes at Glastenbury, and the Professor of Divinity to visit them as often as was convenient. The Seniors, owing to the distraction of the times, were dismissed without the usual public examination and exhibition in July. In September of the same year we find the singular vote, that the College bell may be taken to Glastenbury, if the inhabitants will pay the expense of transportation. This state of dispersion continued through part of the next collegiate year. The Freshmen were not admitted at the proper time on account of the broken state of the College, but in November we find them at Glastenbury with the Juniors. The Senior Class returned to New Haven and were residing there in January, 1778, and in the succeeding June the rest of the students were again collected in their old quarters. In the next winter the ordinary vacation of three weeks was prolonged to seven on account of the steward's inability to procure supplies; and the students were dispersed in the following July, when the British troops invaded New Haven.

The depreciated and fluctuating state of the currency in those times of trial appears abundantly in the financial arrangements of the College. In 1780, for instance, the Corporation voted to reckon all dues paid to the College for the quarter ending December 15, 1779, at thirty-two of paper money for one of silver; from December 15th to January 1st, 1780, at thirty-six for one, and from that time until April 18th, 1780, at forty to one. Salaries were therefore estimated according to the value of several of the principal articles of subsistence. For some years it was the practice to agree with President Stiles, that the prices of beef, pork, wheat and Indian corn were so much, and to bring his salary into the existing currency by this standard. In 1780, the steward was to receive one bushel and one peck of good merchantable wheat, or its equivalent in money, for one week's board. The Professor of Mathematics, in lieu of an order for two hundred and seven pounds in 1778, receives five hundred in 1779, and a Tutor, in the same year, eight hundred and eighty pounds salary. And the expenses of Dr. Stiles's removal from Portsmouth to New Haven amounted to two hundred and forty-two pounds the year before.

In giving these particulars of the disturbed and changeful times in the middle of the war, I have anticipated the appointment of Dr. Stiles to the presidency of the College. His election occurred in September, 1777, but he delayed signifying his acceptance until the following March, and was inaugurated in July. As he was the most learned man of his day in New England, and had kept up a more active intercourse with other learned men than is usual, and withal had lived, all the earlier part of his life, at or near the College; it is not strange that, upon the resignation of Dr. Daggett, many eyes were turned towards him in his distant abode at Portsmouth, New Hampshire, where he took temporary refuge on the occupation of Newport by the enemy. There is evidence that the principal members of the legislature of the state had pitched upon him and expressed their wishes for his election before it was made. The same feeling was shared by important men in Massachusetts, where he had many acquaintances. Thus we find Dr. Chauncey of Boston rejoicing in his appointment and urging him to accept of the office. He was told that nothing but his being a graduate of another institution prevented his election to the presidency of Harvard in 1774. There was, however, apprehension that the Corporation could not be induced to vote for him, for he was regarded as an extremely low Calvinist, and his opinions in respect to ecclesiastical polity differed somewhat from those which prevailed in Connecticut. Yet the choice was effected without much difficulty, and the Fellows gave him their cheerful support; to which they would be the more led, when they came to know him better, by his great sincerity and guilelessness, and by the manifest genuineness of his Christian life. One of his most striking characteristics was ardor and generosity of feeling. This warmth of feeling might perhaps have engendered narrowness of mind, had not skeptical doubts in early life, which were overcome by patient examination of evidence, inclined him to rest upon fundamental points to the disregard of non-essentials; and had not extensive historical knowledge, especially in the department of ecclesiastical history, inclined him to look away from the specific form which theology assumed in his age and country, to the freely changing modifications of a common Christianity. The same warmth of feeling was shown in the ardor with which he, at an early day, espoused the cause of the revolution, and wished to send Christianity to Africa, and to abolish the slave trade. His curiosity was most remarkable. There was no subject which did not interest him, and he dreaded no amount of study in acquiring a new language, or in mastering a new science, or of labor in recording the results of his investigations. It must be said, however, that his mind was not remarkably philosophical. His multifarious knowledge was rather packed together than assimilated, and his style of communicating his thoughts was rather that of one oppressed by the load of his acquisitions than of one who had them under command. His mind inclined strongly to antiquarian researches, and with all his ardor for the new principles of freedom, he loved old usages and forms in academical proceedings. Hence the ancient pomps and customs, the rules of subordination among undergraduates and of etiquette towards the officers at which we now wonder were able to offer some resistance, through his life-time, to the changes of times and of feelings without the College walls. As an instructor he was copious in the information which he conveyed, and enjoyed high respect from his reputation of great learning; but he did not, I suppose, exercise very great sway over the youthful mind, and seems to have been easily deceived, and to have failed in perspicacity. His academical life was past at a time of relaxed morality and of exalted notions of political rights. The religious state of the College was low: sometimes not more than four or five undergraduates were communicants.* And yet the disorders, which might be thought to belong of necessity to such a time, do not seem to have equalled those of the preceding age; owing, perhaps, in part, to the kindliness and freedom from severity of Stiles's character.†

The most important measure of this period has been spoken of in an earlier part of my discourse. I refer to the introduction of new members, eight in number and officers of the state, into the Board of Fellows of the College. The ground which President Clap had taken that the College was entirely independent was good in law but quite unacceptable to many persons in civil life, and was likely to close the public purse to all appeals on behalf of an institution, whose poverty from the first had almost been its destruction. It is probable that many well-wishers to the College, who had no share in its government, thought that some kind of connection with the state would ensure its permanent prosperity, and preserve it from the assaults of men, who were now disposed to attack it on account of its exemption from state control. Nor were the Corporation averse to some arrangement of this description. In the beginning of 1778 they had an interview with a committee of the General Assembly "on the subject of enlarging and extending the plan of education in Yale College." Each party proposed to the other its views and wishes, which were to be discussed at some future meeting. "The committee of the assembly proposed an enlargement of the institution without alteration of charter; that the assembly should give an addition to the library,

* Stiles's Mss., 1779.

† See Appendix, No. XIV.

a philosophical apparatus, and professorships of medicine, law, and oratory, &c., only that they should have a voice in concurrence with the Fellows in appointing professors supported by the state. This they supposed would produce a cordial union between the College and the assembly." Another plan which was suggested by Governor Trumbull was that four civilians should be chosen into the next vacancies in the Corporation. Nothing short of this, he said, would give radical healing and satisfaction. But for a number of years nothing grew out of these projects. In October 1791, a committee was appointed to confer with the President and Fellows of the College in relation to its affairs and to report at the next session. In their report dated May 25, 1792, they say that they found the Corporation disposed to communicate without reserve every circumstance respecting the care and management of the institution under their government. They found that the number of students on an average was about 130, that the severity of the ancient Freshman discipline was almost done away, and that the literary exercises of the respective classes had of late years undergone considerable alterations, so as the better to accommodate the education of the undergraduates to the present state of literature. They further found that the state of the College treasury was in a much better condition than they had apprehended, and that the finances had been managed with great dexterity prudence and economy. After mentioning the amount of funds and of annual expenses, they stated that another building was wanted to accommodate and receive the students, about one half of whom were obliged to furnish themselves with lodgings in the town for want of room in the College, for which purpose, as well as for additions to the library, for the support of a professor of mathematics, and for increase of salaries the help of the legislature was needed. This report, it is said, gratified the legislature; and an act was passed appointing commissioners to receive the balances of taxes laid for the discharge of the principal and interest of the State debt, and to pay over such balances for the use of the College at New Haven, particularly for the erection of a new College building containing students' rooms, and for the purpose of serving as a fund to be applied to the support of professors. The conditions of this grant were that of the sum collected in these balances the College authorities should pay or transfer in legal form to the Treasurer of the state fifty per cent. in some kind of public stock of the United States; and that eight members of the State government, the Governor, Lieut. Governor and six senior assistants in the council, should be *ex officio* members of the Corporation of Yale College, with full powers except as to filling up vacancies in the clerical portion of that body. This act, contemplating a modification of the charter, was accepted not unwillingly by the existing Corporation. With slight alterations, rendered necessary by the new constitution of the State, the relation to the state has continued as was then settled until the present time. The old jealousy of a Corporation for educational purposes managed exclusively by clergymen ceased. The happy adjustment, that neither portion of the body should exercise any control over the election of members pertaining to the other, tended to prevent all jealousy between the orders and to promote union. The civilians infused knowledge of law and of public sentiment into the Board. Their annual election, by giving each predominant political party only a temporary share in the control of the College, really removes it from all undue political influence. In effecting this union Mr. Hillhouse, then and for forty years afterward the Treasurer of the College, had a considerable part. The assistance rendered by this act to the College was of the greatest advantage to its financial interests, perhaps we may say of vital importance; nor could the measures for the increase of instructors and for additions to the buildings, which were carried through in Dr. Dwight's presidency, have been thought of without these very seasonable supplies.

I have now reached a point in the history of the College, where the testimonies of the living and the records of the past touch one another. Of the surviving graduates the oldest proceeded bachelor of arts the very Commencement at which Dr. Stiles was elected to the Presidency, and only about eighty men, the youngest of whom has passed the bounds of threescore and ten, are living witnesses of his times. The venerated and beloved late President of the College left its walls as a student the very year that Dr. Dwight came into office, and the day after his inauguration. From that time onward the voices of the living become numerous and their testimony explicit concerning the College history. Nay, by the kind providence of God, some of those who were at a very early day associated with Dr. Dwight still retain their college posts;—a speaking proof, alike honorable to them and to the institution, of stability in system and permanency of success. The great crowds of living witnesses who advance to meet us from this time onwards, and whose recollections of the past are in many respects more true, and altogether more vivid than any historical records, will supersede the necessity of pursuing this sketch farther. There is another reason also why I might reasonably be silent respecting Dr. Dwight's presidency, for of the subsequent period, and of the living, it would be quite unbecoming to speak. That reason is that being nearly allied by blood to that honored servant of God, and having looked up to him in early youth with the utmost reverence, remembering him as the preacher who first moved my feelings and the adviser who solved my religious doubts and helped my pathway in spiritual things, while yet I was but a child; I would not, if I could, look on his character or his academical policy with the eye of a critic or a historian. Let it suffice to say that if power over the minds of young men, both as a teacher and adviser; if selections of younger colleagues, most completely justified by time and trial; if consecration with religious and self-sacrificing purpose to the interests of the College; if large views as to the plan and extent of education; if the absence of all that was little and selfish; if eloquent earnestness in promoting spiritual interests enforced by a holy life; if these and many other happy characteristics uniting in one college officer make a claim for love and veneration; then the love and veneration which was conceded to Dr. Dwight by contemporaries will not be withheld by posterity, even when recollection shall have become silent in the grave, and the living voice can no longer speak its convictions.

It will be long before the graduates of Yale College will cease to speak of him as

Clarum et venerabile nomen
Gentibus, et nostræ multum quod proderat urbi.

Having now brought this survey of the history of the College down to times embraced with the memories of many, I shall use it as a kind of frame in which may be included some particulars respecting the academical body, the discipline, the instruction, the usages and the structures of the past.

The academical corps concerned in government and instruction was originally designed to consist of a rector and tutors;—the latter, as we have seen, supplying the place of the fellows, who are also tutors, of the colleges of England. Their number has varied from one to five during the last century, and from five to even nine in the present. They were regarded as the nucleus of the college system, so that when a professor of divinity, and afterwards when a professor of mathematics was chosen, tutorial powers were given to them by express vote. After the year 1723, when Rector Cutler conformed to the Church of England, they with the Rector were subjected to a test of the soundness of their Congregational principles. I can find no evidence from the

College records that this test was applied for a number of years, but am not disposed to think that it became obsolete. However this was, in 1753 when the project for establishing a professor of divinity was on foot, a new resolution of the Fellows required that members of their own body with the President, the Professor of Divinity and tutors should give their assent to the Westminster Catechism and Confession of Faith, and should renounce all doctrines and principles contrary thereto, and pass through such an examination as the corporation should order. This new provision for securing orthodoxy was quite unacceptable to a number of educated persons in the Colony, and was one of the causes why President Clap was held in disesteem. It was afterwards modified, in 1778 at the accession of President Stiles, into an assent to the Saybrook Platform; and finally becoming a mere form was abrogated in the year 1823.*

The charter of 1745 imposed another test in the form of a political oath upon all governing officers in the College. They were required before they undertook the execution of their trusts or within three months after "publicly in the college hall [to] take the oaths, and subscribe the declaration, appointed by an act of parliament made in the first year of George the first, entitled an act for the further security of his majesty's person and government, and the succession of the crown in the heirs of the late princess Sophia being Protestants, and for extinguishing the hopes of the pretended Prince of Wales, and his open and secret abettors." We cannot find the motive for prescribing this oath of allegiance and abjuration in the Protestant zeal which was enkindled by the second pretender's movements in England,—for although belonging to this same year 1745 these movements were subsequent to the charter,—but rather in the desire of removing suspicion of disloyalty and of conforming

* At a meeting at Hartford in May, 1823. The writer happened to be the first officer not required by law to make this declaration, having entered the Tutorship in June of that year.

the practice in the College to that required by the law in the English universities. This oath was taken until it became an unlawful one when the State assumed complete sovereignty at the revolution.* For some years afterwards the officers took the oath of fidelity to the State of Connecticut, and I believe that the last instance of this occurred at the very end of the eighteenth century.

Professorships in this College are of subsequent origin to the office of tutors, and the course which things took at Harvard was substantially followed. The first professorship, as was naturally to be expected, was one of divinity, and the next, one of mathematics and natural philosophy. Prof. Daggett the first professor of divinity died in 1780. Two years afterward the Rev. Samuel Wales was appointed his successor. In 1793 in consequence of a mental malady, which had long incapacitated him for business, his office was declared vacant; and after attempts to fill it, extending through several years, Dr. Dwight, then President, was induced to perform its duties, at first upon appointment from year to year, but afterwards as a permanent duty. And this continued to be one of the principal spheres of his efficiency until his death. Dr. Fitch is the fourth in this line of succession which began in 1754. The first professor of mathematics and natural philosophy was appointed in 1770 and resigned his charge in 1781. The office then lay vacant owing to the impoverished state of the College for about three years, during part of which time President Stiles by occasionally lecturing on astronomy discharged a portion of its duties. Just before Dr. Dwight was called to the Presidency this office was again filled, but from financial considerations upon an annual appointment.†

---

* See Appendix, No. XV.

† President Stiles at his own request received the title of professor of ecclesiastical history, and read lectures on the subject, but the office expired with him. It was revived again in 1805 and united with the professorship of languages.

Such was the professorial corps at the beginning of this century—a professor of natural philosophy and mathematics reappointed from year to year, and a professor of divinity who was also President. Dr. Dwight may be said to have given the most important impulse to the College which it ever received, by selecting, soon after the beginning of the present century, several young men who had been already tried in the service of the College, to fill professors' chairs; two of which were newly erected, those of chemistry and of the three learned languages, and one was old, that of mathematics and natural philosophy. Besides these a professor of law read a few lectures in the first ten years of the century, and the Medical Department was founded in 1813. Since the death of Dr. Dwight the growth of the College has been more manifested by providing instruction in new branches, and by subdividing professorial departments than in any other way.* The professorship of mathematics has been separated from that of natural philosophy, that of Greek from that of Latin; and the new chairs of Rhetoric and of Mental and Moral Philosophy,—the latter upon a foundation provided by a bequest,—have been established; while the three new faculties of Theology, Law and of Philosophy,—the first embracing three, the second two, and the latter three professorships not included in the other departments,—have been begun within a few years.† Thus the institution called a College really consists of five faculties; several of which are indeed in their incipient state, and almost or entirely unendowed, and therefore not sure of permanence; but all are in successful operation.

With the College authorities according to the first idea are to be numbered as having subordinate executive powers, the monitors, the scholar of the house, the beadle, and the butler. The name of monitor sufficiently explains the office to

---

* See Appendix, No. XVI.

† A professorship of Natural History was established the day before this discourse was delivered.

those who are acquainted with college affairs. The scholar of the house,—scholaris ædilitius of the Latin laws—before the institution of Berkeley's scholarships which had the same title, was a kind of ædile appointed by the President and tutors to inspect the public buildings, and answered in a degree to the Inspector known to our present laws and practice. He was not to leave town until the Friday after Commencement because in that week more than usual damage was done to the buildings. The beadle or his substitute the vice-beadle (for the sheriff of the county came to be invested with the office,) was the master of processions, and a sort of gentleman-usher to execute the commands of the President. He was a younger graduate settled at or near the College. There is on record a diploma of President Clap's, investing with this office a graduate of three years standing, and conceding to him "omnia jura privilegia et auctoritates ad Bedelli officium, secundum collegiorum aut universitatum leges et consuetudines usitatas, spectantia." The office, as is well known, still exists in the English institutions of learning, whence it was transferred first to Harvard and thence to this institution.

The classes since 1817, when the office of butler was abolished, are probably but little aware of the meaning of that singular appendage to the College, which had been in existence a hundred years. To older graduates the lower front corner room of the old middle College in the south entry must even now suggest many amusing recollections. The butler was a graduate of recent standing, and being invested with rather delicate functions was required to be one in whom confidence might be reposed. Several of the elder graduates who have filled this office are here to-day, and can explain, better than I can, its duties and its bearings upon the interests of College. The chief prerogative of the butler was to have the monopoly of certain eatables, drinkables and other articles desired by students. The Latin laws of

1748 give him leave to sell in the buttery cider, metheglin, strong beer to the amount of not more than twelve barrels annually,—which amount as the College grew was increased to twenty,—together with loaf sugar ('saccharum rigidum'), pipes, tobacco and such necessaries of scholars as were not furnished in the commons hall. Some of these necessaries were books and stationery, but certain fresh fruits also figured largely in the butler's supply. No student might buy cider or beer elsewhere. The butler too had the care of the bell and was bound to wait upon the President or a Tutor and notify him of the time for prayers. He kept the book of fines, which as we shall see was no small task. He distributed the bread and beer provided by the steward in the Hall into equal portions, and had the lost commons, for which privilege he paid a small annual sum. He was bound in consideration of the profits of his monopoly to provide candles at college prayers and for a time to pay also fifty shillings sterling into the treasury. The more menial part of these duties he performed by his waiter.

The original motives for setting up a buttery in colleges seem to have been to put the trade in articles which appealed to the appetite into safe hands, to ascertain how far students were expensive in their habits, and prevent them from running into debt; and finally by providing a place where drinkables of not very stimulating qualities were sold to remove the temptation of going abroad after spirituous liquors. Accordingly laws were passed limiting the sum for which the butler might give credit to a student, authorizing the President to inspect his books, and forbidding him to sell anything except permitted articles for ready money. But the whole system, as viewed from our position as critics of the past, must be pronounced a bad one. It rather tempted the student to self-indulgence by setting up a place for the sale of things to eat and drink within the College walls, than restrained him by bringing his habits under inspection. There was nothing to prevent his going abroad in quest of stronger drinks than could be bought at the buttery, when once those which were there sold ceased to allay his thirst. And a monopoly, such as the butler enjoyed of certain articles, did not tend to lower their price, or to remove suspicion that they were sold at a higher rate than free competition would assign to them.

In speaking of the collegiate discipline and instruction in past times it will be proper to preface our remarks with a few words relating to the ancient laws, which are our principal sources of information upon these points. It might be expected that the usages of Harvard would be followed by men who had received their education at that earlier fountain of knowledge in New England; and it will seem natural also to find a general conformity between the methods of study and government there and in the colleges of Oxford and Cambridge. In the very first year of the legal existence of the College we find the Trustees ordaining that, "until they should provide further, the Rector or Tutors should make use of the orders and institutions of Harvard College, for the instructing and ruling of the collegiate school, so far as they should judge them suitable, and wherein the Trustees had not at that meeting made provision." The regulations then made by the Trustees went no further than to provide for the religious education of the College and to give to the College officers the power of imposing extraordinary school exercises or degradation in the class. The earliest known laws of the College belong to the years 1720 and 1726, and are in manuscript; which is explained by the custom that every Freshman, on his admission, was required to write off a copy of them for himself, to which the admittatur of the officers was subscribed. In the year 1745 a new revision of the laws was completed which exists in manuscript; but the first printed code was in Latin and issued from the press of T. Green at New London in 1748. Various editions with sundry changes in them appeared between that time and the year 1774, when the first edition in English saw the light. It is said of this edition that it was printed by particular order of the legislature. That honorable body, being importuned to extend aid to the College, not long after the time when President Clap's measures had excited no inconsiderable ill-will, demanded to see the laws; and accordingly a bundle of the Latin laws,—the only ones in existence,—were sent over to the state house. Not admiring legislation in a dead language, and being desirous to pry into the mysteries which it sealed up from some of the members, they ordered the code to be translated. From that time the numberless editions of the laws have all been in the English tongue.

It would be an interesting task, did time permit, to gather the progress of legislation from a comparison of the laws at different times. Nothing would place in a clearer light the change in usages and in the method of discipline, which gradually came about after the death of President Clap, and especially after the American revolution. But all that we can do within our limits is to invite attention to a few characteristic points.

The old system of discipline may be described in general as consisting of a series of minor punishments for various petty offences, while the more extreme measure of separating a student from College seems not to have been usually adopted until long forbearance had been found fruitless, even in cases which would now be visited in all American colleges with speedy dismission. The chief of these punishments named in the laws are imposition of school exercises—of which we find little notice after the first foundation of the College, but which we believe yet exists in the colleges of England; deprivation of the privilege of sending Freshmen upon errands, or extension of the period during which this servitude should be required beyond the end of Freshman year; fines either specified of which there are a very great number in the earlier laws, or arbitrarily imposed by the officers; admonition and degradation. For the offence of mischievously ringing the bell, which was very common whilst the bell was in an exposed situation over an entry of a college building, students were sometimes required to act as the butler's waiters in ringing the bell for a certain time. Of fines the laws are full, and other documents show that the laws did not sleep. Thus there was in 1748 a fine of a penny for the absence of an undergraduate from prayers, and of a half-penny for tardiness or coming in after the introductory collect; of fourpence for absence from public worship; of from two to six pence for absence from one's chamber during the time of study; of one shilling for picking open a lock the first time and two shillings the second; of two and sixpence for playing at cards or dice or for bringing strong liquor into College; of one shilling for doing damage to the College or jumping out of the windows,—and so on in many other cases.

In the year 1759, a somewhat unfair pamphlet was written, which gave occasion to several others in quick succession, wherein amidst other complaints of President Clap's administration, mention is made of the large amount of fines imposed upon students. The author, after mentioning that in three years' time over one hundred and seventy-two pounds of lawful money was collected in this way, goes on to add that "such an exorbitant collection by fines tempts one to suspect that they have got together a most disorderly set of young men training up for the service of the churches, or that they are governed and corrected chiefly by pecuniary punishments;—that almost all sins in that society are purged and atoned for by money." He adds with justice that these fines do not fall on the persons of the offenders,—most of the students being minors,—but upon their parents; and that the practice takes place chiefly where there is the least prospect of working a reformation, since the thoughtless and extravagant, being the principal offenders against College law, would not lay it to heart if their frolicks should cost them a little more by way of fine. He further expresses his opinion that this way of punishing the children of the College has but little tendency to better their hearts and reform their manners; that pecuniary impositions act only by touching the shame or covetousness or necessities of those upon whom they are levied; and that fines had ceased to become dishonorable at College, while to appeal to the love of money was expelling one devil by another, and to restrain the necessitous by fear of fine would be extremely cruel and unequal. These and other considerations are very properly urged, and the same feeling is manifested in the laws by the gradual abolition of nearly all pecuniary mulcts. The practice, it ought to be added, was by no means peculiar to Yale College, but was transferred, even in a milder form, from the colleges of England.

The punishment of degradation, laid aside not very long before the beginning of the revolutionary war, was still more characteristic of the times. It was a method of acting upon the aristocratic feelings of family; and we at this day can hardly conceive to what extent the social distinctions were then acknowledged and cherished. In the manuscript laws of the infant college we find the following regulation which was borrowed from an early ordinance of Harvard under President Dunster. 'Every student shall be called by his sir name except he be the son of a nobleman, or a knight's eldest son.' I know not whether such a 'rara avis in terris' ever received the honors of the College; but a kind of colonial untitled aristocracy grew up composed of the families of chief magistrates, and of other civilians and ministers. In the second year of College life precedency according to the aristocratic scale was determined, and the arrangement of names on the class roll was in accordance. This appears on our triennial catalogue until 1768, when the minds of men began to be imbued with the notion of equality. Thus for instance, Gurdon Saltonstall, son of the governor of that name, and descendant* of Sir Richard, the first emigrant of the family, heads the class of 1725, and names of the same stock begin the lists of 1752, and 1756. It must have been a pretty delicate matter to decide precedence in a multitude of cases, as in that of the sons of members of the council or of ministers, to which class many of the scholars belonged. The story used to circulate, as I dare say many of the older graduates remember, that a shoemaker's son, being questioned as to the quality of his father, replied, that *he was upon the bench*, which gave him of course a high place. Now such being the principle of rank, degradation consisted in placing a student on the list, in consequence of some offence, below the level to which his father's condition would assign him; and thus declared that he had disgraced his family. This seems to have been a somewhat severe punishment, and one not often inflicted.

There was a still more remarkable punishment, as it must strike the men of our times, and which, although for some reason or other no traces of it exist in any of our laws so far as I have discovered, was in accordance with the 'good old plan,' pursued probably ever since the origin of universities. I refer,—'horresco referens,'—to the punishment of boxing or cuffing. It was applied before the Faculty to the luckless offender by the President, towards whom the culprit, in a standing position, inclined his head, while blows fell in quick succession upon either ear. No one seems to have been served in this way except Freshmen and commencing 'Sophimores.'† I do not find evidence that this usage much survived the first jubilee of the College. One of the few known instances of it, which is on other accounts remarkable, was as follows: a student in the first quarter of

* i. e., Great-great-grandson. The order was, 1. Sir Richard, 2. Richard, 3. Nathaniel, 4. Gurdon, 5. Gurdon.

† See note to Appendix, No. XVII.

his Sophomore year, having committed an offence for which he had been boxed when a Freshman, was ordered to be boxed again, and to have the additional penalty of acting as butler's waiter for one week. On presenting himself, more academico, for the purpose of having his ears boxed, and while the blow was falling, he dodged and fled from the room and the College. The beadle was thereupon ordered to try to find him and to command him to keep himself out of College and out of the yard, and to appear at prayers the next evening there to receive further orders. He was then publicly admonished and suspended; but in four days after submitted to the punishment adjudged, which was accordingly inflicted, and upon his public confession his suspension was taken off. Such public confessions, now unknown, were then exceedingly common.

Nor ought my hearers to marvel at this practice, seeing that bodily punishments were part and parcel of the original system of college discipline. May I be permitted to give one or two proofs of this assertion. In the laws of Harvard, which were in force in 1739,* and how much later I know not, occurs the following rule: "notwithstanding the pecuniary [fines] it shall be lawful for the President, Tutors or Professors to punish undergraduates by boxing when they judge the nature and circumstances of the offense call for it." In the seventeenth century the discipline at Harvard proceeded to much greater lengths than this. In 1674, a student who had uttered "blasphemous words" was by sentence—not of the Faculty or Corporation but—of the Overseers, publicly whipped before all the scholars, besides being subjected to other penalties and indignities.† The English practice revealed at least an equal degree of severity. The excerpts from the body of Oxford statutes printed in the very year when this College was founded, threaten corporal

* I quote from a Ms. copy written out that year.

† Pierce's Hist. Harv. Univ., p. 227. Quincy's id. 1, 189.

punishment to persons of the proper age,—that is below the age of eighteen,—for a variety of offences; and among the rest for disrespect to Seniors, for frequenting places where 'vinum aut quivis alius potus aut herba Nicotiana ordinarie venditur,' for coming home to their rooms after the great Tom or bell of Christ's Church had sounded, and for playing foot-ball within the University precincts or in the city streets. But the statutes of Trinity College, Cambridge, contain more remarkable rules, which are in theory still valid, although obsolete in fact.* All the scholars, it is there said, who are absent from prayers,—bachelors excepted,—if over eighteen years of age "shall be fined a half-penny, but if they have not completed the year of their age above mentioned they shall be chastised with rods in the hall on Friday." At this chastisement all undergraduates were required to be lookers on, the Dean having the rod of punishment in his hand; and it was provided also that whosoever should not answer to his name on this occasion, if a boy, should be flogged on Saturday. No doubt this rigor towards the younger members of the society was handed down from the monastic forms which education took in the earlier schools of the middle ages. And an advance in the age of admission, as well as a change in the tone of treatment of the young may account for this system being laid aside at the Universities; although as is well known, it continues to flourish at the great public schools of England.†

The inquiry may here arise, what was the behavior of the Yale College student a century ago compared with that in the present generation. This enquiry is a difficult one to answer, because nothing is more fleeting and changing than

---

* Dean Peacock's observations on the statutes of the University of Cambridge, p. 122.

† I have been informed by one of his scholars that Dr. Arnold was extremely rigorous in discipline, and even flogged the boys of the sixth form with a cane himself.

college manners, which fluctuate perceptibly from year to year, and receive their direction, it may be,—especially in a small college,—from one or two leading students. I have had access to some written documents which supply the materials for a judgment as to this point, and yet perhaps the times to which they refer may have been no fair specimen of the average of college history. Taking however these into connection with the recollections of elderly men relating to a more recent period, we seem to be able to form a conclusion on pretty sure grounds that there has been a gradual improvement, if not in deference of manners, at least in morals and deportment; that there is not more vicious indulgence now, if as much, as when the number of students was half as large; that boyish turbulence and noise have somewhat abated and given place to a more gentlemanly style of behavior; and that coarse conduct and low tricks of mischief have in a good degree ceased. I believe that the experience of others among the older colleges coincides with this result. This may be ascribed to a more general refinement in society, to a greater number of religious students leavening the mass, to the temperance reformation, and to improvements in college government. And it holds out a cheering prospect for the future, if such a tendency reaching through many years may be discovered.

In connection with the subject of discipline we may aptly introduce that of the respect required by the officers of the College, and of the subordination which younger classes were to observe towards older. The germ and perhaps the details of this system of college manners is to be referred back to the English universities. Thus the Oxford laws require that "Juniors shall show all due and befitting reverence to Seniors, that is undergraduates to Bachelors, they to masters, masters to Doctors, as well in private as in public by giving them the better place when they are together, by withdrawing out of their way when they meet, by uncovering the head at the proper distance and by reverently saluting and addressing them." The Harvard laws express themselves thus upon this subject. "All scholars shall show due respect and honor in speech and behavior to the President and Fellows of the Corporation, and to all others concerned in the instruction and government of the college, and to all superiors, keeping due silence in their presence and not disorderly gainsaying them, but showing to them all expressions of honor and reverence that are in use, such as uncovering the head, rising up in their presence and the like; and particularly undergraduates shall be uncovered in the college yard when any of the overseers, the President, or Fellows of the Corporation, or any others connected in the government or instruction of said college are therein, and bachelors of arts shall be uncovered when the President is there." Our laws of 1745 contain the same identical provisions. These regulations were not a dead letter, nor do they seem to have been more irksome than many other college restraints. They presupposed originally that the college rank of the individual towards whom respect is to be shown could be discovered at a distance by peculiarities of dress: the gown and the wig of the President could be seen far beyond the point where features and gait would cease to mark the person. When the outward badges of academic dignity fell into disuse, the minute etiquette above spoken of fell with it: or rather both owed their decline together to that feeling of democratic equality introduced by the revolution, which greatly narrowed the intervals between different ages and conditions; which brought down the ministers from their somewhat lordly bearing; which unclothed judges of their gowns; and which, if united to a gentlemanly sense of propriety, gives rise to the best of all stiles of manner, because the freest expression of the sentiments; but if united to a brutish and arrogant self-valuation, must destroy the decencies of society and even deprave morals.

Another remarkable particular in the old system here was the servitude of Freshmen,—for such it really deserves to be called. The new comers,—as if it had been to try their patience and endurance in a novitiate before being received into some monastic order,—were put into the hands of the Seniors to be reproved and instructed in manners, and were obliged to run upon errands for the members of all the upper classes. And all this was very gravely meant and continued long in use. The Seniors considered it as a part of the system to initiate the ignorant striplings into the college system, and performed it with the decorum of dancing masters. And, if the Freshmen felt the burden, the upper classes who had outlived it and were now reaping the advantages of it, were not willing that the custom should die in their time.

The following paper, printed I cannot tell when, but as early as the year 1764,* gives information to the Freshmen in regard to their duty of respect towards the officers, and towards the older students. It is entitled "FRESHMAN LAWS," and is perhaps part of a book of customs which was annually read for the instruction of new comers.†

"It being the duty of the Seniors to teach Freshmen the laws, usages and customs of the College, to this end they are empowered to order the whole Freshman class, or any particular member of it, to appear, in order to be instructed or reproved, at such time and place as they shall appoint; when and where every Freshman shall attend, answer all proper questions, and behave decently. The Seniors, however, are not to detain a Freshman more than five minutes after study-bell, without special order from the President, Professor or Tutor."

"The Freshmen, as well as all other undergraduates, are to be uncovered, and are forbidden to wear their hats (unless in stormy weather) in the front door-yard of the President's or Professor's

---

* The name of Seth Hunt, a graduate of 1768, is written on one extant copy.

† Stiles' diary, June 29, 1778. "This evening I began to read the book of customs in the Chapel."—Less remarkable portions of the paper are omitted.

house, or within ten rods of the person of the President, eight rods of the Professor, and five rods of a Tutor.

"The Freshmen are forbidden to wear their hats in College-yard (except in stormy weather, or when they are obliged to carry something in their hands) until May vacation; nor shall they afterwards wear them in College or Chapel.

"No Freshman shall wear a gown, or walk with a cane, or appear out of his room without being completely dressed, and with his hat; and whenever a Freshman either speaks to a superior or is spoken to by one, he shall keep his hat off, until he is bidden to put it on. A Freshman shall not play with any members of an upper class, without being asked; nor is he permitted to use any acts of familiarity with them, even in study-time.

"In case of personal insult a Junior may call up a Freshman and reprehend him. A Sophimore in like case must obtain leave from a Senior, and then he may discipline a Freshman, not detaining him more than five minutes, after which the Freshman may retire, even without being dismissed, but must retire in a respectful manner."

"Freshmen are obliged to perform all reasonable errands for any superior, always returning an account of the same to the person who sent them. When called, they shall attend and give a respectful answer; and when attending on their superior, they are not to depart until regularly dismissed. They are responsible for all damage done to any thing put into their hands, by way of errand. They are not obliged to go for the undergraduates in study-time, without permission obtained from the authority; nor are they obliged to go for a graduate out of the yard in study-time. A Senior may take a Freshman from a Sophimore, a Bachelor from a Junior, and a Master from a Senior. None may order a Freshman in one play-time, to do an errand in another."

"When a Freshman is near a gate or door, belonging to College or College yard, he shall look around, and observe whether any of his superiors are coming to the same; and if any are coming within three rods, he shall not enter without a signal to proceed. In passing up or down stairs, or through an entry or any other narrow passage, if a Freshman meets a superior, he shall stop and give way, leaving the most convenient side—if on the stairs the bannister side. Freshmen shall not run in College yard, or up or down stairs, or call to any one through a College window. When going into the chamber of a superior, they shall knock at the door, and shall leave it as they find it, whether open or shut. Upon entering the chamber of a superior, they shall not speak until spoken to; they shall reply modestly to all questions, and perform their messages decently and respectfully. They shall not tarry in a superior's room, after they are dismissed, unless asked to sit. They shall always rise, whenever a superior enters or leaves the room, where they are, and not sit in his presence until permitted.

"These rules are to be observed not only about College, but everywhere else within the limits of the City of New Haven."

This is certainly a very remarkable document, one which it requires some faith to look on as originating in this land of universal suffrage, in the same century with the declaration of independence. He who had been moulded and reduced into shape by such a system might soon become expert in the punctilios of the court of Louis XIV.

This system however had more tenacity of life than might be supposed. In 1800 we still find it laid down as the Senior's duty to inspect the manners and customs of the lower classes and especially of the Freshmen; and as the duty of the latter to do any proper errand, not only for the authorities of the College but also, within the limits of one mile, for resident graduates and for the two upper classes. By degrees the old usage sank down so far, that what the laws permitted was frequently abused for the purpose of playing tricks upon the inexperienced Freshmen; and then all evidence of its ever having been current disappeared from the College code. The Freshmen were formally exempted from the duty of running upon errands in 1804.

The laws are also our most important guide in regard to the studies and the system of instruction. Here, if anywhere, there has been change and growth. Yet it is often difficult to trace the changes, and to discover the course which instruction has taken from age to age. In general it may be said that the system pursued by the earlier teachers rested upon logic and theology, and presupposed that the students would choose the clerical profession, rather than the offices of civil life. To this cause is to be ascribed the part which the study of Hebrew played for a considerable period. Another point aimed at then but neglected since was the ready speaking and writing of Latin. On the other hand I cannot find that the mathematical sciences received much attention before the time of President Clap; rhetoric was but little cultivated until a few years before the revolution; the physical sciences which rest on experiment were entirely unknown until a later period; and the study of Greek was confined to the New Testament. To mention the sciences then untaught, which have grown up at this seat of learning since the beginning of the present century, would be to repeat what has already been said of the enlargement of the academic body.

The religious turn which the first founders aimed to give to the teachings in their Collegiate School, appears from the preamble of the very first act of theirs on record after the charter. This, although it has been published before, is too important not to find a place here. "Whereas," say they—in a most sincere religious spirit, and with a deep sense of the greatness of the work for which they were girding themselves,—"whereas, it was the glorious public design of our now blessed fathers, in their removal from Europe into these parts of America, both to plant, and under the divine blessing to propagate in the wilderness the blessed reformed Protestant religion, in the purity of its order and worship, not only to their posterity but also to the barbarous natives,—in which great enterprise they wanted not the royal commands and favor of his majesty Charles the Second to authorize and invigorate them,—we, their unworthy posterity, lamenting our past neglect of this grand errand, and sensible of our great obligations better to prosecute the same, and desirous in our generation to be serviceable thereunto,—whereunto the liberal and religious education of suitable youth is under the blessing of God a chief and most profitable expedient,—therefore do in duty to God and the weal of our country undertake in the aforesaid design."

These feelings were not dictated by fear of a rival Protestant sect, and then expressed under the form of zeal for religion,—for none existed or was apprehended within the Colony;—nor did they spring from that intense dislike of Romanism, which Protestants have sometimes shown in its presence and where it is growing; but they were, I do not doubt, prompted by a large and pure love of religion, which, though they might regard their own way as greatly the best, yet looked not on it as an end, but as a means of promoting a common Christianity.

The following also is part of a very early resolution: "that the Rector shall take effectual care that the students be weekly called memoriter to recite the Assembly's Catechism in Latin, and Ames' theological theses, of which as also of Ames' cases he shall make or cause to be made from time to time such explanations, as may be through the blessing of God most conducive to their establishment in the principles of the Christian protestant religion."

The old manuscript laws of 1720 and 1726 give the following account of the studies pursued in the College. The system, no doubt, closely resembled that which was in vogue then and at an earlier date at Harvard, where all the original Trustees but one and the earliest Rectors and Tutors received their education. "In the first year after admission, on the four first days of the week, all students shall be exercised in the Greek and Hebrew tongues only; beginning logic in the morning at the latter end of the year, unless their Tutors see cause by reason of their ripeness in the tongues to read logic to them sooner. They shall spend the second year in logic with the exercise of themselves in the tongues; the third year principally in physics, and the fourth year [in] metaphysics and mathematics, still carrying on the former studies. But in all classes the last days of the week are allowed for rhetoric, oratory, and divinity." Another law of the same code will best describe these last mentioned studies. "All students shall, after they have done reciting rhetoric and ethics on Fridays, recite Wollebius' theology; and on Saturday morning they shall recite Ames' theological theses in his Medulla, and on Saturday evening the Assembly's Shorter Catechism in Latin, and on Sabbath day morning attend the explanation of Ames' cases of conscience." And another law ordains that "all undergraduates shall publicly repeat sermons in the hall in their course, and also bachelors; and be constantly examined on Sabbaths [at] evening prayer." With regard to practice in the learned languages, particularly the Latin, it is prescribed that "no scholar shall use the English tongue in the College with his fellow scholars, unless he be called to a public exercise proper to be attended in the English tongue, but scholars in their chambers, and when they are together shall talk Latin." And again all undergraduates except Freshmen, who shall read English into Greek, shall read some part of the Old Testament out of Hebrew into Greek in the morning, and shall turn some part of the New Testament out of the English or Latin into Greek at evening at the time of recitation, before they begin to recite the original tongues."* With regard to public exercises it is said that "all students in the school shall observe their courses for disputations; Bachelors once every week and the

* The meaning of this probably is that a verse of the English Testament shall be turned memoriter into Greek, of the Hebrew Scriptures into Septuagint Greek, and so a verse of some Latin version of the New Testament into the original.

undergraduates, after they have begun to learn logic, five times every week, except six weeks for the commencers* before and one month for the rest of the students after Commencement. Likewise all undergraduates shall declaim once in two months."

The Latin laws published in 1748, of which also an English original under date of 1745 is extant in manuscript, prescribe that in the first year the students "shall principally study the tongues and logic, and shall in some measure pursue the study of the tongues the two next years. In the second year they shall recite rhetoric, geometry and geography. In the third year natural philosophy, astronomy and other parts of the mathematics. In the fourth year metaphysics and ethics.—Every Saturday shall especially be devoted to the study of divinity, and the classes through the whole term of their College life, shall recite the Westminster Confession of Faith received and approved by the churches in this Colony, Wollebius', Ames' Medulla, or any other system of divinity by the direction of the President and Fellows. And on Friday each undergraduate in his order, about six at a time, shall declaim in the Hall in Latin Greek or Hebrew, and in no other language without special leave, and the two Senior classes shall dispute twice a week."

As President Clap stood high in his day for attainments in the mathematical sciences, and indeed was selected to fill the place of Rector on that account, it was natural that he should give an impulse to these branches of study. Such appears to have been the case, if we may rely on tradition and on his own account of the matter in his history written in 1766,—the year of his resignation. He there says of the studies in general that the scholars at their admission "are able well to construe and parse Tully's orations Virgil and the Greek Testament, and understand the rules of common arithmetic. In the first year they learn Hebrew, and prin-

* i. e., The Seniors after their examination for degrees.

cipally pursue the study of the languages, and make a beginning in logic and some parts of the mathematics. In the second year they study the languages; but principally recite logic, rhetoric, oratory, geography and natural philosophy; and some of them make good proficiency in trigonometry and algebra. In the third year they still pursue the study of natural philosophy, and most branches of mathematics. Many of them well understand surveying, navigation and the calculation of eclipses; and some of them are considerable proficients in conic sections and fluxions. In the fourth year they principally study and recite metaphysics, ethics and divinity.—The two upper classes exercise their powers in disputing, every Monday in the syllogistic form, and every Tuesday in the forensic."—"The President frequently makes public dissertations upon every subject necessary to be understood to qualify young gentlemen for [the] various stations and employments [of civil life,] such as the nature of civil government, the civil Constitution of Great Britain, the various kinds of courts,—the several forms of ecclesiastical government which have obtained in the Christian church," etc.

From this account it may be gathered that the mathematics had come to occupy some of the space, which was given at first to logic. In the life of Dr. Dwight by his son it is stated, that ten years after this he carried his class as far as any of them would go into the Principia of Newton. This however must have been a very rare thing. The first mathematical work of which I can find traces—and for this information as well as for much relating to the course of study I am indebted to Prof. Kingsley—was Ward's mathematics which contains a meagre collection of the most elementary propositions in geometry and in conic sections. Rohault's, and in President Clap's time Martin's philosophy in three volumes was the text-book for that science; when this work came to be out of print, President Stiles by advice of

Dr. Price procured Enfield's philosophy to be imported and made use of it; which was the first introduction of that now obsolete text-book into the American colleges. In the earliest times of the College it seems that a manuscript text-book of natural philosophy was prepared by Rector Pierson, which the students were expected to copy. Perhaps also the first text-books in logic were manuscript before either Ramus or Burgersdicius was used: on ethics a treatise was written by President Clap, which served the purposes of the College for a considerable time. The Latin authors studied in College were chiefly Virgil, Horace and Cicero de Oratore. No Greek beyond the New Testament is known to have been taught to the classes in regular course until after the present century began.*

The fluent use of Latin was acquired by the great body of the students: nay certain phrases were caught up by the very cooks in the kitchen.. Yet it cannot be said that elegant Latin was either spoken or written. There was not, it would appear, much practice in writing this language, except on the part of those who were candidates for Berkleian prizes. And the extant specimens of Latin discourses written by the officers of the College in the past century are not eminently Ciceronian in their style. The speaking of Latin, which was kept up as the College dialect in rendering excuses for absences, in syllogistic disputes, and in much of the intercourse between the officers and students, became nearly extinct about the time of Dr. Dwight's accession. And at the same period syllogistic disputes, as distinguished from forensic, seem to have entirely ceased.

An impulse was given to the study of English literature by some of the younger officers of the College about the beginning of the revolution. In 1776 we find the Seniors petitioning that Mr. Dwight—then Tutor—might instruct

---

* See Appendix, No. XVII.

them in rhetoric, history and belles lettres. This movement is worthy of notice as indicating the commencement of another period, when the English mother tongue was more valued, because it expressed the fervid feelings of souls aroused and exalted by the impending revolution. It was coeval also with the first poetic attempts of a school nearly confined to graduates of this College, such as Trumbull, Dwight, Humphreys and Barlow, who if they reached not a high point of poetic merit, failed not in fervent sympathy for whatever was great and good. Their inspiration was the same which was felt at Lexington and at Bunker's Hill.

If you compare the old system of study according to this sketch with that which has by degrees grown up since the accession of Dr. Dwight, we shall find great advances in the later period. More of mathematics,—if we measure by thorough prosecution rather than by number of branches,—is studied in the Freshman year than formerly during the whole course: the study of natural philosophy has made great progress; that of chemistry and natural history is wholly modern; metaphysical and political science have assumed a new importance in the College course; the same is true of rhetoric; modern languages had then no provision made for them whatever;* and more Greek is required now for entering than was then acquired before graduation. We see and acknowledge defects; and yet we may say with Homer's Sthenelus but in no boastful spirit,

ἡμεῖς τοι πατέρων μέγ' ἀμείνονες, εὐχόμεθ' εἶναι.

And yet that old system in which dry logic formed the staple is not to be despised, for by it some of New England's best minds were formed. It is remarkable that nearly all the fathers and choir-leaders of what may technically be called New England theology came from this College. Men like Jonathan Edwards, Bellamy, Hopkins, West, Smalley, and

* See Appendix, No. XVIII.

Emmons,—graduates of the years between 1720 and 1770, —do not proceed from cloistered retirements, where the mind is wholly asleep, and afraid to think. And whether we admit their conclusions or not, we must admit that they are close consecutive reasoners, always in earnest, who take broad views of the divine government over the universe, and cover up deep religious emotions under logical forms.

On the other hand an effect of the modern system of education or of society or of both is to repress originality of thinking, to destroy individual peculiarities, and to produce a general sameness among those who are educated. One is often reminded of Dr. Arnold's complaint that there were few in his school who rose above the general average, no great geniuses or young persons of extraordinary abilities. Our schools are like our political systems, and our fashions; the training and curbing power of the mass upon the individual is quite as remarkable, as the raising of the general standard. Our abundance of books too anticipates and prevents the free movements of thought; so that while learning has undoubtedly increased and with it the power of correct expression, and some in younger classes now could rebuke graduates of honor of former days for slips and errors in knowledge, we miss free and elastic minds rejoicing in their own movements and working fearlessly for themselves the mines of truth.

The system of education thus imperfectly sketched continued as now through four years; for although a very early act of the original Trustees contemplates granting a diploma of Bachelor after three years residence to students of distinguished industry and ability, and of Master after two years more upon the same terms, I do not find that this thought was ever carried into effect. The examinations for degrees then as now* took place in July, but examinations were very

* An alteration or precession of the terms ordered this year may bring it into June.

light compared with the present system. Commencements were not to be public according to the wishes of the first Trustees, through fear of the attendant expense; but another practice soon prevailed, and continued with three or four exceptions until the breaking out of the war in 1775. They were then private for five years on account of the times. The early exercises of the candidates for the first degree were a "saluting" oration in Latin, succeeded by syllogistic disputations in the same language; and the day was closed by the master's exercises,—disputations and a valedictory. According to an ancient academical practice theses were printed and distributed upon this occasion, indicating what the candidates for a degree had studied, and were prepared to defend; yet, contrary to the usage still prevailing at universities which have adhered to the old method of testing proficiency, it does not appear that these theses were ever defended in public. They related to a variety of subjects in Technology, Logic, Grammar, Rhetoric, Mathematics, Physics, Metaphysics, Ethics, and afterwards Theology. The candidates for a master's degree also published theses at this time, which were called Quæstiones magistrales. The syllogistic disputes were held between an affirmant and respondent, who stood in the side galleries of the church opposite to one another, and shot the weapons of their logic over the heads of the audience. The saluting bachelor and the master who delivered the valedictory stood in the front-gallery, and the audience huddled around below them to catch their Latin eloquence as it fell. It seems also to have been usual for the President to pronounce an oration in some foreign tongue upon the same occasion.*

At the first public Commencement under President Stiles in 1781, we find from a particular description which has been

* The earliest theses extant belong to 1714, and the last were printed in 1797. From 1787 onwards there were no Masters' valedictories, nor syllogistic disputes in Latin, and in 1793 there were no masters' exercises at all.

handed down, that the original plan, as above described, was subjected for the time to considerable modifications. The scheme in brief was as follows: the salutatory oration was delivered by a member of the graduating class, who is now our aged and honored townsman Judge Baldwin. This was succeeded by the syllogistic disputations, and these by a Greek oration, next to which came an English colloquy. Then followed a forensic disputation in which James Kent was one of the speakers. Then President Stiles delivered an oration in Hebrew, Chaldaic and Arabic,—it being an extraordinary occasion,—after which the morning was closed with an English oration by one of the graduating class. In the afternoon the candidates for the second degree had the time, as usual, to themselves, after a Latin discourse by President Stiles. The exhibitors appeared in syllogistic disputes, a dissertation, a poem and an English oration. Among these performers we find the names of Noah Webster, Joel Barlow and Oliver Wolcott. Besides the Commencements there were exhibitions upon quarter days, as they were called, in December and March, as well as at the end of the third term when the younger classes performed; and an exhibition of the Seniors in July, at the time of their examination for degrees, when the valedictory orator was one of their own choice.* This oration was transferred to the Commencement about the year 1798, when the Masters' valedictories had fallen into disuse; and being in English gave a new interest to the exercises of the day.

Commencements† were long occasions of noisy mirth, and even of riot. The older records are full of attempts, on the part of the Corporation, to put a stop to disorder and extravagance at this anniversary. From a document of 1731 it appears that cannons had been fired in honor of the day, and stu-

---

* See Appendix, No. XIX.

† This and the eight following paragraphs were omitted in the public delivery of this discourse for want of time.

dents were now forbidden to have a share in this on pain of degradation. The same prohibition was found necessary again in 1755, at which time the practice had grown up of illuminating the College buildings upon Commencement eve. But the habit of drinking spirituous liquor and of furnishing it to friends on this public occasion grew up into more serious evils. In the year 1737 the trustees, having found that there was a great expense in spirituous distilled liquors upon Commencement occasions, ordered that for the future no candidate for a degree or other student should provide or allow any such liquors to be drunk in his chamber during Commencement week. And again it was ordered in 1746, with the view of preventing several extravagant and expensive customs, that there should be "no kind of public treat but on commencement, quarterdays, and the day on which the valedictory oration was pronounced; and on that day the Seniors may provide and give away a barrel of metheglin and nothing more." But the evil continued a long time. In 1760 it appears that it was usual for the graduating class to provide a pipe of wine, in the payment of which each one was forced to join. The Corporation now attempted by very stringent law to break up this practice; but the Senior class having united in bringing large quantities of rum into College, the Commencement exercises were suspended, and degrees were withheld until after a public confession of the class. In the two next years degrees were given at the July examination with a view to prevent such disorders, and no public Commencement was celebrated. Similar scenes are not known to have occurred afterwards, although for a long time that anniversary wore as much the aspect of a training day, as of a literary festival.

The Commencement day in the modern sense of the term, —that is a gathering of graduated members and of others drawn together by a common interest in the College and in its young members who are leaving its walls,—has no counterpart that I know of in the older institutions of Europe. It arose by degrees out of the former exercises upon this occasion, with the addition of such as had been usual before upon quarter days, or at the presentation in July. For a time several of the commencing masters appeared on the stage to pronounce orations, as they had done before. In process of time, when they had nearly ceased to exhibit, this anniversary began to assume a somewhat new feature; the peculiarity of which consists in this, that the graduates have a literary festival more peculiarly their own, in the shape of discourses delivered before their assembled body or before some literary society.

A historical sketch of Yale College would not be complete without embracing an account of the library, the apparatus in natural science, and the buildings. The two former are chiefly of modern growth, and their increase from almost nothing has been followed up by many living witnesses. And one of the principal contributions to the library in early times has already been incidentally noticed. I will therefore confine myself to a few words on the history of the College buildings.

There was a house at Saybrook owned by the Collegiate School, where probably recitations were heard and the library was deposited.* But it contained no accommodations for students' lodgings, which served as a principal argument for the removal of the institution to another quarter.

The circumstances under which the first College at New Haven was erected, and the ceremonies with which it was

* Mr. Noyes of Lyme in his memorial to the legislature in 1717 says, "I am not satisfied that the charter doth grant power to the Trustees to remove the school after such a settlement made as was at Saybrook. For that would infer that they might leave it in that estate forever. They had a house there, though not so great as that frame at New Haven."

President Stiles also, in his oration at laying the foundation stone of Union Hall now called South College, speaks of a small college domicile erected for its use at Saybrook.

called after Gov. Yale have already been detailed. This building was of wood and was situated near the corner of College and Chapel streets about twenty feet from the former. It was one hundred and seventy feet long twenty-two wide and three stories high and contained in its three entries a Hall, a Library and twenty students' rooms, in which seventy students could be packed together. This original namesake of Yale lasted sixty-five years and was taken down, when now almost a ruin, in 1782.

In 1745, upon a representation by President Clap that this College building was inadequate to hold the students, the General Assembly granted a lottery for the purpose of building another. The lottery yielded five thousand and two hundred pounds old tenor, and subsequent donations chiefly from the same source amounted to nearly fifteen thousand more. But this sum ought, I believe, to be divided by twelve to reduce it to pounds sterling. The edifice constructed with these proceeds was intended to be one hundred and five feet long, forty wide and three stories high, besides containing garrets and a cellar with compartments for each room. It was called Connecticut Hall, and was situated near the north end of the College yard. It was finished as to its exterior in 1752, but was not ready for habitation before 1756. In 1797 a fourth story was built upon it in lieu of the attic, and it now stands, thus transformed, the oldest monument upon our grounds, under the name of South Middle College.

This building contained only rooms for students. The Hall in the older College was used for religious services, for lectures and for commons. It was not strange therefore that in 1760 a new building was projected, which should contain a Chapel and a Library. This structure, is the Chapel known to all the graduates now living down to 1824, but has long since ceased to fulfill its original destination,—the Library having been removed to the room now known as the Rhetorical Chamber in 1804, and the new

Chapel having been built on account of the insufficient size of the old one twenty years afterward. In 1782 a vote was passed to build a Hall and kitchen of brick, one story high with a cellar under the whole. This building answered its purpose until 1819, when the new Hall with the Cabinet room over it was erected, and the old one was turned into a Laboratory. The building now called South College, but at first named Union Hall in consequence of the union of clerical and lay members in one Corporation, was commenced in 1793. The original plan for this building contemplated placing it to the north of the existing College, and at right angles to it; but the present design and site were afterwards adopted. The erection of the Lyceum and the North Middle College or Berkeley Hall belong to the very commencement of the present century. The line of buildings was continued afterwards at times which many here present will readily recall. Of the less inelegant buildings in the rear of the main line I need not speak, as their date is within the reach of younger memories; nor have I time to do more than hint at the gradual acquisition, especially since 1795, of portions of the square where the Colleges are situated, until a year or two since, the whole plot came into the hands of the Corporation in full ownership.

In this sketch of the College buildings we have made reference to three successive Commons' Halls, the most recent of which has been devoted to another use in consequence of the abandonment of the system of Commons some ten years since. At first a College without common meals was hardly conceived of; and indeed if we trace back the history of colleges as they grew up at Paris, nothing is more of their essence than that students lived and eat together in a kind of conventual system. No doubt also when the town of New Haven was smaller, it was far more difficult to find desirable places for boarding than at present. But however necessary, the steward's department was always beset with difficulties and exposed to complaints which most gentlemen present can readily understand. The following rations of commons voted by the Trustees in 1742 will show the state of College fare at that time. "Ordered that the steward shall provide the commons for the scholars as follows viz. for breakfast, one loaf of bread for four, which [the dough] shall weigh one pound. For dinner for four, one loaf of bread as aforesaid, two and a half pounds beef, veal or mutton, or one and three quarter pounds salt pork about twice a week in the summer time, one quart of beer, two pennyworth of sauce [vegetables]. For supper for four, two quarts of milk and one loaf of bread when milk can conveniently be had, and when it cannot then apple-pie, which shall be made of one and three fourth pounds dough, one quarter pound hog's fat, two ounces sugar and half a peck apples." In 1759 we find, from a vote prohibiting the practice, that beer had become one of the articles allowed for the evening meal. Soon after this the evening meal was discontinued, and, as is now the case in the English colleges, the students had supper in their own rooms, which led to extravagance and disorder. In the revolutionary war the steward was quite unable once or twice to provide food for the College, and this as has already appeared led to the dispersion of the students in 1776, and 1777, and once again in 1779 delayed the beginning of the winter term several weeks. Since that time nothing peculiar has occurred with regard to commons, and they continued with all their evils of coarse manners and wastefulness for sixty years. The conviction meanwhile was increasing that they were no essential part of the College, that on the score of economy they could claim no advantage, that they degraded the manners of students and fomented disorder. The experiment of suppressing them has hitherto been only a successful one. No one who can retain a lively remembrance of the commons and the manners as they were both before and since the building of the new Hall in 1819 will wonder that this resolution was adopted by the authorities of the College. And it is to be hoped and supposed, if some greyhaired man forty or fifty years hence shall be describing at one of these anniversaries the burschen-like doings of the Commons' Hall in his day, that this will seem to the young men of the time as marvellous a thing as the servitude of the Freshmen which has been spoken of, and as exploded as to take the oath of allegiance to the house of Hanover.

Such, gentlemen, are some of the particulars which I thought you would be interested in having laid before you, well aware as I am that the time which you can spare from the remaining festivities of the day forbids any thing more than a meagre outline. But I shall be satisfied, if there be awakened in your minds a desire to have the history of Yale College given to the world on a larger scale than has been hitherto attempted. I should be happy if such a desire on your part could lead to such an undertaking one who has thoroughly explored our records, who has already sketched a brief outline of our annals, and whose caution united to acuteness render his investigations worthy of all confidence. From him, whose society has been one of my highest enjoyments during my academical life, I have derived much information, which I could obtain from no other source; and he has guided me to documents of which few persons know the existence. May his life be lengthened out in a cheerful old age, and may he be disposed to occupy a portion of his leisure in performing the office of historian of the College to which its authorities long since invited him.

And will not this historical sketch be admitted to have shown great change and progress in our College affairs? Of proofs of change indeed the whole history of the College has been full. Whether we compare the usages of the olden time with those of the present, or the discipline, or the studies, or the means by which improvement can be effected, or the standard of scholarship, or the number of officers employed in educating, or the numbers educated, everywhere we see change marked and sweeping; so that he, who should join together in his mind the first period of the College at Saybrook, or even its first age at New Haven, with the actual state at this day, without knowing the transitions, might reasonably doubt its identity. These changes, moreover, must be regarded as progress, not as a backward course. For not only have they been introduced in order to come nearer to the best standard of education; but they have justified themselves by the confidence of discerning persons, and by increased numbers and efficiency. Far be it from me indeed, in adducing increased numbers as a proof of true progress, to express the opinion that numbers are any evidence, when two institutions are compared, of superiority in the one over the other. The highest style of education is not needed in this country, and if offered, would not be accepted. There are many reasons, too, besides merit, why one institution should be thronged, while another makes a show of empty benches. But this I would say, that an increase in this respect running through a long course of years is a proof that no radical vice of management has disclosed itself, and that the permanent art is possessed of gaining public confidence. And if this enlargement should be found united with changes which were intended to be improvements, then the two concurrent things,—the professed improvements and the increase,—would speak favorably for each other.

It is sometimes said by persons who look with a jealous eye on colleges, particularly on their social and political influences, that they are immovable institutions, conservative of knowledge elsewhere useless and forgotten, opposed to new science, to the practically useful and the popularly intelligible. But the sketch which I have laid before you, fellow graduates, suffices, if any thing were needed, to show how unjust and one-sided are these allegations. True it is that colleges are not apt to think that

> " Of old things all are over old,
> Of good things none are good enough,"

nor to overturn instead of repairing. A confession of past failure and ill-success, such as that implied in revolutionary measures of destruction and renovation, is not apt to be made by them, or to express their convictions. But then the changes, great as they may seem if measured by the contrasts of centuries, are no violent nor sudden ones: they are such changes as time with his gentle irresistibleness works in whatever is not made but grows; in states and churches, and all things which live not by infusion and propping up but by inward energy. If the past may be our rule of judging we shall have such changes still. They will come, as they have come, through enlightened men in colleges and enlightened graduates without their walls. But far be from us those changes which instead of ingrooving themselves in forms becoming obsolete* tear and snap in twain; those which break up the flow of College history; which sever the connection with past science and with the world of the past; which render the venerable forms of grey antiquity less venerable to the scholar; which make a gap in the long procession of science upon which ages have looked as spectators, and inspire the student with the conceit that he is not at all a transmitter and a torchbearer, but rather one of a new race the creators and sole possessors of knowledge.

The strength and much of the use of a literary institution depends upon its antiquity and the stability of its system. From the regular progress of centuries it acquires a reputation which its officers are ashamed to fall below; and a set

---

* " Let the change which comes be free
To ingroove itself with that which flies."—*Tennyson.*

of maxims and principles resembling the habitual rules of a well principled man. Its students come into sympathy with its eminent graduates of the past, and take upon themselves something of the dignity,—the ἀξίωμα, which those confer upon their place of education. When we reflect that Harvard was founded before any chartered body in this land, and that since the origin of Yale College nearly all the states of Europe and America have been unmade and made over; it will not seem strange that membership in such a society has a powerful though a silent influence on character, to give value to objects of reverence, and to oppose violent and sudden innovation. The very existence of society depends on regard for that which is established. If the family ties had no more binding force, if love for *our* country as a complex existence in the past had ceased, what State could be sure of lasting through a generation. So also the love felt towards an ancient seat of learning by its sons tends to make them, while they rejoice in every improvement, dread whatever threatens to overthrow it or alter its identity. There may be new institutions better than Yale:—we claim no superiority nor suppose that we have reached perfection. But we love our College better than we can some result of modern experiment, because it is venerable, because it is deserving of love and because it is ours. Thus I suppose that there are no men in our land more conservative, in the best sense, than thoughtful graduates especially of the older institutions. They are men on whom such institutions may rely in hours when speculative projects and theories of half-education are popular, and whose approbation outweighs the whole voice of the public besides.

Indeed, gentlemen, may I not say in this hour devoted to our Alma Mater that her reliance must be preëminently on her graduated sons. Situated in a state and town which are not opulent, having projects and reasonable wants which far outrun its resources, where can it turn but to those three thousand living graduates, whose very number, caused by its reputation, is some proof that that reputation has not been ill-founded. As we review its past history we find it constantly struggling with poverty, and sometimes near to extinction. Will the year 1900 see it still in the same plight; or will those who have watched it, as it strove almost beyond its strength to keep on the upper level of education, feel the spirit of foster sons, and help its advancement by their τροφεῖα. For advance it must, or lose its relative importance; since every where institutions of learning are groping or intelligently climbing, full of resources and of youthful hope, towards the highest style of education.*

This day which reminds us of the goodly throng of our fellow-graduates, and of the support which the College hopes and expects from them, reminds us also of one painful subject. These graduates are disappearing from the stage of life; and I doubt not that those, who have from year to year listened to the catalogue of deaths, have been saddened amid their pleasant recognitions and their revived recollections of College scenes, at the thought that so many of the wise and good are annually passing away. For one I am pained to to feel that the objects which my youth revered are almost gone, that the pinnacles of society to which I lifted up my eye are levelled with the dust; and a distressing want has arisen within me,—which affects me however reflection may pronounce it to be delusive,—as if men were beginning to have less of manhood and less of power than heretofore. Since the last triennial was issued and before the present year, such important names as James Kent, Jeremiah Mason, Samuel Hubbard, Timothy Pitkin and Jabez W. Huntington have been numbered with the dead. The present year also has to mention names of worth and honor freshly marked with stars. Of this number it may fall to another's province

---

* See Appendix, No. XX.

before the day is out to crown with just eulogy that eminent southern statesman, whose depth of thought and earnest purpose, united to large political experience disinterestedness and independence, gave him unlimited sway over the minds of such as embraced his views of the Constitution. To another of this year's deceased graduates, eminent in his profession of the law but unversed in political life, may I as to a revered friend and preceptor be allowed to pay in passing a brief tribute of honor. Charles Chauncey of Philadelphia was one whom any college might feel proud to number among its sons. Long among the leaders of the bar, a man of the kindest disposition, one of the truest gentlemen that ever lived,—to these qualities he added sterling worth built upon Christian principle, and might be held up as a model to all young men entering his profession, to teach them that there is something better than political power, to which he never aspired, or than wealth which he scattered with a liberal hand; that the affections of fellow-citizens will cling to a man who lives not for himself; and that no dignity conferred by men is as high as that of the Christian gentleman.

Such are some of the painful thoughts, which crowd into the mind to-day. But I turn, gentlemen, to the future in confident hope that the graduates of coming years will acquit themselves as worthily as those of the past have done; and that still, as long as the College, the country and time shall last, men of power and goodness will point hither with pride as to their place of education. And may not an augury be taken for the future progress of the College from the past? May we not infer from the living force which she has shown and from her gradual growth that there are no seeds of decay in her,—that the purposes she answers, the wants she supplies are not those of an age or a clique but of human improvement throughout time. With good auguries and hopes then we send her on her course through the next fifty years. But I would rather change the tone of augury and prophecy into prayer and say : may those who shall assemble here then see improvement and growth as great as we can trace since the commencement of the century. Before that time may her inelegant buildings give place to structures worthy to be the home of learning, and representing to the eye in form and material an institution calculated for all time. May her resources be adequate to every healthy enlargement. May her officers be every way abler and better than the best of their predecessors. May her students be industrious, thoughtful, earnest *men,* in whom solid well disciplined minds and characters shall be the foundation and assurance of success in life. Above and before all may GOD BE PRESENT to give light and to leaven with his holy influence all study and all discipline. But if,—which may he avert,—she should desert his ways, and give herself up to evil and to falsehood, I pray not for her prosperity :—I rather pray that she may fall.

APPENDIX.

No. I.

THE proceedings at the celebration of the third jubilee since the founding of Yale College, held August 14, 1850, were as follows.

The graduates assembled in the College Chapel were called to order about half-past nine o'clock; when Prof. SILLIMAN, Sen., (graduate of 1796,) was appointed the President of the day, A. N. SKINNER, Esq., Mayor of New Haven, (1823,) the Vice President, and SAMUEL H. PERKINS, Esq., of Philadelphia, (1817,) and Rev. S. W. S. DUTTON, of New Haven, (1833,) the Secretaries. The latter gentleman then read the proceedings of last year's meeting of the graduates, and the obituary notices of graduates, who have deceased since the last Commencement. Upon this a procession in order of Collegiate age,—the longest ever known at Yale College, and consisting probably of more than a thousand graduates besides invited strangers,—was formed to the first Church, where, after a prayer by Rev. Dr. Cooley, of Granville, Mass., (1792,) the present discourse was delivered. On returning to the College the company was almost immediately summoned to a collation. The tables were arranged in front of the Library under tents disposed in the form of a triclinium with a marquee tent in the center. Around the marquee were placed portraits of former officers and benefactors of the College with the name of each inscribed in letters of leaves; and above, encircling the tent, the motto of the College seal, *Lux et Veritas*. The tables were decorated with flowers. About one thousand persons partook of the repast. The company consisted of graduates arranged together according to classes, so that familiar faces could greet one another, of benefactors to the College, and of other invited guests, among whom were officers of a number of literary institutions.

After the collation was ended the President of the day, Prof. Silliman, made a brief address to the company as a preface to the subsequent proceedings; in which he mentioned that having given notice in 1849, after fifty years of official duty, of his purpose to retire from his post at this Commencement, he had been led by the request of the authorities of the College to withdraw his resignation. He then announced the first toast, 'Yale College,' which was responded to in a brief speech by Ex-President Day, (1795.) The next sentiment, 'Harvard, our elder sister,' called up Prof. Felton of that University. The third, 'our alumni of the Clergy,' was answered by Rev. Dr. Bacon of New Haven, (1820.) The fourth, 'our alumni of the Bench and Bar,' brought out Daniel Lord, Esq., of New York, (1811,) and Dr. Alexander H. Stevens of the same city, (1807,) spoke to the fifth, 'the alumni of the Medical profession.' The Hon. Edward Bates of Missouri spoke to the sixth toast, 'Westward the star of empire takes its way,' and Prof. Brown, of Dartmouth, to a sentiment in which his College was honorably mentioned. The Rev. John Pierpont, (1804,) then read a poem on 'Progress,' which was well received by the audience. The 'Poets of America,' were toasted, and Dr. Oliver W. Holmes a Professor in Harvard responded in a few lines. The concluding sentiment was 'our alumni of the South,' to which William T. Gould, Esq., of Augusta, Georgia, (1816,) responded, taking occasion to pay a tribute of praise to Mr. Calhoun who died within the year.

During the course of this meeting, were sung several pieces, written for the occasion, in which the 'Beethoven Society,' of the undergraduates, with some graduates who had been members of the same, lent very efficient aid. Together with these were sung those four verses of the sixty-fifth Psalm in Sternhold and Hopkins' version, which were sung at the Commencement of 1718. The company broke up about six o'clock.

No. II.

The commemoration here referred to consisted in nothing more than a Latin discourse pronounced on Commencement day in September, 1752, by Ezra Stiles then Senior Tutor. The discourse which is still preserved among his papers is in indifferent Latin, and is occupied partly with a summary view of the history of the College. The 'Old Middle' was then in building. 'Qui præ me' says he speaking of President Clap, 'laudes [ejus] dixere, Bibliothecæ catalogum, legumque non scriptarum et statutorum Yalensium Collectiones, perpetua [ejus] de academia curæ monumenta, memorarunt. His adde sortilegium nov-academicum et alios mille modos quibus largissimos nummos gazophylacio nostro annumeravit ad erigendum conficiendumque novum Academiæ domicilium, quod sexto Aprilis (1750,) undecimo præsidiatus [ejus] anno inceptum, jam ferme confectum videmus.' The reference in the word 'sortilegium' is to the lottery granted by the State for building the new College in May, 1747, from which source five thousand two hundred pounds old tenor or about four hundred and thirty-three pounds sterling (?) came into the College treasury.

The first diploma of Yale College was of this form. We take it from a copy in President Stiles' diary.

Omnibus et singulis has literas lecturis Salutem in Domino. Vobis notum sit Quod Stephanum Buckingham, candidatum secundum in artibus gradum desiderantem, tam probavimus quam approbavimus. Quem examine et tentamine prævio approbatum nobis placet titulo et gradu artium liberalium magistri adornare et decorare. Cujus hoc instrumentum in membrana scriptum testimonium sit. A gymnasio Academico in Colonia Connecticutensi, Nov-Anglia. Datum Say-Brookei decimo sexto Calendarum Octobris [!]; Anno Domini MDCCII.

Abrah. Pierson, *Rector*.
James Noyes, }
Noadiah Russel, } *Inspectores*.
Samuel Russel, }

No. III.

Dr. Trumbull in his history of Connecticut (Vol. I, pp. 450, 451) pronounces the number of inhabitants in the Colony in 1717 to be seventeen thousand. The area of the Colony as yet incorporated was divided into four counties, of which Hartford comprised beyond its present bounds part of Middlesex, all of Tolland that was then incorporated and portions of Windham, together with the town of Waterbury; while New London took in Saybrook and Killingworth beyond the river, and Voluntown and Pomfret which were afterwards set off to Windham. To New Haven pertained Durham and the very new settlement of New Milford. This will help the reader to understand the remonstrance of the inhabitants of Hartford and New London counties complaining that the interests of those the largest counties were not considered in removing the College to New Haven.

No. IV.

This Appendix contains

(1.) Proposals for erecting a University, etc.

(2.) Letter of Increase Mather without address, dated Sept. 15, 1701.

(3.) Two letters of Judge Sewall to Rev. James Pierpont, dated Sept. 17, 1701, and Oct. 29, 1701.

(4.) Letter of Messrs. Sewall and Addington, dated Oct. 6, 1701.

(5.) Their draft of a charter for the College in Connecticut, transmitted with the foregoing letter.

(6.) The original charter of the College, passed Oct. 9, 1701.

(7.) Remarks on the preceding papers.

(1.)

Proposals for erecting an University in the renowned Colony of Connecticut, humbly offered by a hearty (tho' unknown) well-wisher to the welfare of that religious Colony.

I. Let there be called a Synod of all the consociated churches in this Colony.

The Synod (or council of elders and messengers from the churches,) may as yet be called by the civil government, upon the motion of some eminent pastors. Or, if that way should fail, why may not as many of the Pastors, as can come together, modestly write a circular letter unto the churches, intimating their desire of their sending their delegates unto a Synod, (at a proper time and place agreed on,) upon this great occasion of settling an University, for the propagation of literature and religion among them.

II. The Synod being assembled, let the work of that venerable assembly be to resolve upon an University, that shall be the school of the churches, and upon the laws by which the said University shall be governed.

Let these laws declare what shall be the qualifications of them that shall be admitted into the Society; what shall be the studies therein followed and how managed; what shall be the names of the students and how rewarded or censured; and upon what accomplishments the persons there educated shall go forth with ample testimonials recommending them to the acceptance of the world.

III. We cannot presume to give degrees pro more Academiarum in Angliâ, nor are the degrees of Bachelor of Arts and Master of Arts, in the forms they are now ordinarily given, much more than empty titles. A diploma or testimonial (signed by the President and the Tutors of the University and by three of the Inspectors) asserting the qualifications of him that receives it, will be as good as a degree in the honorable thoughts of reasonable men. And, it is hoped, a society of such persons, thus founded and formed, may without presumption give such a testimonial unto those that shall under their education deserve it.

If the young gentlemen will not be satisfied without titles equivalent unto a Baccalaureus and Magister, it will be easy to gratify them. He that goes forth, qualified with a Testimonial, and intending the service of the churches may be stiled *instructus ecclesiæ*. He that goes forth, intending to serve his country in any other capacity but that of a divine may be stiled *ornatus patriæ*: (suppose the word *servus* understood.) But let the President and the Tutors with the Inspectors, appoint still what time they please, in the year, for solemn and rigid Examen, of those that are the *candidates of approbation*.

Let it be considered whether the time for the scholars going forth *Instructi* or *Ornati* should be limited unto the term of their continuance four or five or more years under their education. Would it not be better for the rules of qualification to be sufficiently strict and fixed? And then, a scholar that shall come up to them sooner may go forth an *Instructus* or *Ornatus* with an earlier harvest of his diligence. And the slothful or stupid may stay, as 'tis fit they should, until their merits may challenge their testimonial.—But then the *Examen* must be impartial.

IV. Let the Synod choose at least the first President. If it seem too great a trouble for the churches to come together, as often as a successor may be to be chosen; Quære, whether the Inspectors may not be trusted with the choice. Only then let the Inspectors write letters to all the consociated churches, reporting *whom* they have elected, and *how* and *why*. And if one third of the Churches do signify by letters to the Inspectors that they do not approve of their action let them proceed unto another election.

Quære, whether the President must always be chosen for life, (or at least quamdiu se bene gesserit,) or, whether (at least upon the difficulty of obtaining a more continued supply,) an eminent pastor may not be borrowed for four or five years from his church; and his church be in the meantime supplied with candidates of the ministry: the President himself coming to them as often as may be to dispense all special ordinances.

The work of the President shall be ordinarily once a day to entertain the scholars in a public hall with prayers, and such other exercises, whether expositions of the scriptures, or lectures in divinity, or church history, or somewhat else, as may be most serviceable; and frequently to examine the conduct of the Tutors, and the progress of the scholars; and execute the discipline of the University, according to the laws of it; and preach publicly in the University-town as often as he can.

To such encumbrances, and such entertainments will the President be obliged, that he must have a considerable salary. Until those methods be taken, (which may soon be taken,) whereby such a salary may be raised; why may not the synod resolve that each of the consociated churches do its part; and that it shall be treated as a censurable scandal, for every particular person under the church-watch, to refuse to do his duty in the general contribution? It will be so little among so many churches and persons, that it will be scarce felt by any but such as are of a very quick sense in such matters.

V. Let the Pastors of such twelve churches as the Synod shall pitch upon, be for the time being the stated Inspectors of the University; and every seven of those twelve be a Quorum. Only let none be allowed for to act as Inspectors, until they subscribe certain articles, relating to the purity of religion, that shall be by the Synod agreed upon. And let none be allowed as President or Tutors without subscribing those articles. Let the inspectors visit the University twice at least in a year, and assist the President in regulating all things, not only then but also as often as he shall send for them.

Two tutors may be enough at first. But how shall they be maintained? Some way must be thought of that the public may pay for their board; some such way as that which provides a salary for the President. For their further subsistence let there be a convenient sum set upon the heads of all that are under their tuition.

VI. There have been many famous universities which have had no colleges. Yea, one of the most famous universities now in Europe hath seven or eight hundred students in it; and yet they have no collegiate way of living, but board here and there in the town, where they can. There needs but one large room for the stated meetings of all the scholars.

The Synod shall determine the town that shall be the seat of the University. By all means let it be a seaport town.

The scholars may board at houses in the town, where they may be best provided for. Only, let not the scholars board in any families but such as the pastor and other officers of the church may under their hands allow, as fit, (in regard of their exemplary piety,) for that service of boarding young men that are to be the hope of the flock. Let the president and inspectors of the University limit and retrench the price of boarding, if any of the inhabitants begin to oppress the students in the matter.

If these, or the like proposals may be received by a colony famous for true religion, and in which there are many pious and prudent gentlemen, who can't but foresee the vast consequences of such an undertaking, as is here proposed; there yet remain many considerable things, to be humbly offered, relating to the laws of their University, when there shall be, (which the Lord grant,) an happy opportunity for it.

[This is directed to the Reverend,

Mr. Noyes, of Stonington,
Mr. Buckingham, of Saybrook,
Mr. Pierpont, of New Haven.

On the back is written by some one " A scheme for a College, 1700." And also " instructions for a collegiate school."]

(2.)

Letter of Increase Mather.

Boston, Sept. 15, 1701.

Rev. and Dear Sir,—Not long since a minister in your Colony was pleased to desire my advice concerning an Academical School designed to be erected in your Colony. I shall suggest a few particulars to you.

In the universities in Holland and other foreign countries they do not live a collegiate life but board in the town where the Academy is. By taking this course you may save more than a

£100 in building a house. Only 'tis necessary there should be a large room hired to attend disputations, orations and other public exercises.

A President and two or three Tutors may be sufficient for the ordinary good government of your school in Academical learning. If for the making of laws, election of officers, &c., there shall be seven Inspectors appointed, it may do well; especially if these be the pastors of the next neighboring churches.

Public commencements in our college have of late years proved very expensive, and are occasion of much sin. That may [be] done privately as well as publicly. At some times in the universities of England they have no public acts, but give degrees privately and silently.

The presidents and professors in the protestant (?) universities in France were maintained by the churches: and the several churches were directed by the synods what they should contribute in order thereto.

If the Connecticut government, before their charter is taken from them, shall settle (?) a revenue for the maintainance of such a school, 'tis probable that property will not be taken from you, though government should.

These things are what, at present, occur to my thoughts, which, (as also what I have written to Mr. Buckingham of Seabrook,) take in good part. I commend you and your undertaking, (in which the welfare of your Colony and posterity is greatly concerned,) to the grace of Christ, and remain, Sir,

Yours to my power,
I. MATHER.

(3.)

For the Rev. Mr. James Pierpont at New Haven.

Boston, Sept. 17, 1701.

Sir,—The letter subscribed by Mr. Chauncey, Buckingham, Pierson, Pierpont and Saltonstall, bearing date Aug. 7th, came to hand, Aug. 26. And your own, dated Aug. 26, I received Sept. 13th, at my return from Bristow. I gave the enclosed to the Secretary, and we conferred notes. But it has been a very hurrying time with us by reason of the Governor's power being devolved on the Council, and the setting of the general Court the beginning of this month.

I have been thinking that considering the present distress, it may be best to do as little by the government as is possible with attaining the end. And therefore should not be eager in building a college or settling revenues by a law. But let the scholars board in the town, as it is in Holland : and only build a hall with chamber over it for a library. Unless you can hire a large house that may accommodate the President and those ends also. And so let the act only contain authority for such a person by himself and Tutors under him to instruct youth in academical learning, and give them degrees, as the late reverend and godly learned Mr. Charles Chauncey was wont to do at Cambridge in New England, and as was accustomed to be done under his presidentship. And all persons admitted to any degrees shall have the same honor and respect shown them that students have or ought to have had at Harvard College from the said Charles Chauncey, or from any other President before or after him in Harvard College at Cambridge aforesaid. And let the act oblige the president to pray and expound the Scriptures in the hall, morning and evening de die in diem, and ground the students in the principles of religion by reading to them or making them recite the Assembly's Confession* of Faith, which is turned into good Latin, as also the Catechises, and Dr. Ames' Medulla. And the students shall obey the president and tutors, and conform themselves to such wholesome orders as shall be appointed, subscribing them at their entrance. And let the entire course of academical exercises be maintained and the performance of them exacted with all imaginable strictness and severity, without dispensation to any.

Mr. Secretary presents his service to you, and the gentlemen you joined with in your above mentioned letter. We account our-

---

* I mention the Confession of the Assembly of Divines, because Arminianism is crept even into the Dissenter's annotations, as may be seen upon Heb. ii, 9, said to be done by Mr. Obadiah Hughes.

selves honored in that you have imparted to us a matter of so great concernment, and hope within these few days to send you something more mature and in form either by the post or some other good hand. I have enclosed for each of you my small essay towards opening the eighteenth century; and a sheet to discourage our trading to Africa for men. It is a pity that in New England any should defend and plead for slavery with that rigor as they do.

As for news I cannot learn that the danger is yet over of our being all slain at once by act of Parliament, nulling the American charters. By the prorogation of the Parliament all bills must determine: but they may be received at the next meeting, if they please. There is a further settlement of the crown by act of Parliament upon the princess Sophia electress dowager of Hanover, daughter of the queen of Bohemia, and on her heirs; none being or turning or marrying a papist to inherit the crown. June 10th, 1701, at Kensington, his electoral highness of Hanover was elected a Knight Companion of the most noble order of the Garter. Thos. A. B. [archbishop of] Canterbury, Sir Nathan Wright, keeper, Thomas Earl Pembroke, President Council, William Duke Devonshire, Steward, Charles Duke Somerset, Edward Earl Jersey, Chamberlain, and Sidney Lord Godolphin, First Lord Commissioner of the Treasury, were appointed Lords justices of England upon the King's going into Holland. Sir Thomas Trevor is made Lord chief justice of the common pleas in the place of Sir George Treby, deceased. And Edward Northey, Esq., of the Middle Temple, is made Attorney General. All grandees of Spain are to be dukes and peers of France; and all dukes and peers of France are to be grandees of Spain. The match seems to proceed between the King of Spain and Duke of Savoy's daughter, which makes me fear lest Geneva be not at last broken in upon. Count Staremberg, famed for defending Vienna in 1688, is dead. It is said the emperor's army have had a battle with the French in their passage into Italy, and the Imperialists have had the best of it by much.

As to our affairs, it is said that Col. Dudley has an order signed by the King to be our Governor; that Sir Henry Ashhurst and two more with him oppose it: they pleaded the taking off Governor

Leisler, and the disaffection of the people to him, for the demonstration of which they produced a letter under the hand of four of the Council here. Papers made use of before the Lords Justices were sent over to the King in Holland. Mr. Jer. Dummer writes that this opposition will not avail, and that Col. Dudley will be our Governor, and be with us before we are aware.

My humble services to you and the gentlemen concerned with you and to Mrs. Pierpont, from, Sir, your humble servant,

SAMUEL SEWALL.

From the same to the same.

Boston, Oct. 29, 1701.

Sir,—Your letters of the 15th and 16th inst. are come to hand which gave Mr. Addington and me a great deal of pleasure, to see that you had so soon got an act passed for the erecting of a College in your Colony: and to have Mr. Buckingham's own hand as a sure testimony of his being alive; after the rumor which we had of his being dead; which made us sad.

It would be an ample reward of any thing we have done for you, if you would send us a fair authentic copy of the act, which we desire; as also of the place where the College is to be, so soon as you have appointed it.

Mr. William Atwood had yesterday his commission for being Judge of the Admiralty read in council; and then he took the oaths, and subscribed the declaration and association to qualify himself to enter upon the exercise of his authority here. Byfield and Winthrop are both alike laid aside now, and that authority, which is, we know not how large, passed over into other hands.

Gillam is not arrived, so that we are longing to hear more news from England, and yet afraid at the same time what we shall hear. Gwin come in from Lisbon reports, that a fleet of ours of fifty-two ships from sixty to eighty guns, six fire-ships and four bomb-ketches was seen not far from Cape Finisterre. It is much mused whither they be bound, and on what design. The Hamburger that fell among them, and brought news of it to Lisbon they obliged him to separate from them, not suffering him to remain in the fleet. This fleet was seen about the middle of August. This snowy day is designed for the ordination of Mr. Blowers at Beverly.

Present our hearty service to Mr. Chauncey, Buckingham, Pierson and Saltonstall.

Mr. Timothy Woodbridge remains lame here by reason of a humor fallen into his right leg. We are generally in health.

I am, Sir, your servant,

SAMUEL SEWALL.

(4.)

Letter of Messrs. Sewall and Addington.

Boston, Oct. 6th, 1701.

Gentlemen,—We crave your pardon that we have made you wait so long for so little. We might frame an excuse from the present circumstances of affairs and say *multa nos impedierunt.* But there is another cause that made us slow and feeble in our progress, not knowing what to do for fear of overdoing. And that is the reason there is no mention made of any visitation, which is exceedingly proper and beneficial; all humane societies standing in need of a check upon them. But we knew not how to call or qualify it, but that in a little time it might probably prove subversive of your design. We on purpose gave your academy as low a name as we could, that it might the better stand in wind and weather, not daring to incorporate it, lest it should be liable to be served with a writ of *quo warranto.*

We pray you to accept of the few inclosed minutes for an act, and should have travelled further in it, if your instructions or our invention had dictated to us, not knowing well what scheme to project, because we could not tell how far your government will encourage the design.

We should be very glad to hear of flourishing schools and a College at Connecticut, and it would be some relief to us against the sorrow we have conceived for the decay of them in this province. And as the end of all learning is to fit men to search the Scriptures, that thereby they may come to the saving knowledge of God in Christ; we make no doubt but you will oblige the Rector to expound the Scriptures diligently morning and evening.

Praying God to direct and bless you beyond what yourselves do understand or hope for, we take leave and remain

Your affectionate and humble servants,

SAM. SEWALL,

ISA. ADDINGTON.

[Addressed to "Mr. THOMAS BUCKINGHAM, Minister of the Gospel at Saybrook."

President Quincy has published this letter without date in the Appendix (No. XXVII) to the first volume of his History of Harvard. He says, "the date of this letter is wanting in the copy, but it must have been written about the end of 1700 or the beginning of 1701." The real date, as we see, places it towards the end of 1701, which is important as showing that there was no long consultation with the Massachusetts gentlemen prior to the charter.]

(5.)

Charter drafted by Sewall and Addington before the revisions and alterations of the Trustees.

Connecticut in New England,—An act for founding a Collegiate School. Whereas several well disposed and public spirited persons, of their sincere regard to, and zeal for the upholding and propagating of the Christian Protestant religion, by a succession of learned and orthodox men, have expressed their earnest desires that a collegiate school be founded and suitably endowed within this his Majesty's Colony of Connecticut, for the educating and instructing of youth in good literature, arts and sciences, that so by the blessing of Almighty God, they may be the better fitted for public employment both in the church and in the civil state; and have manifested their willingness to contribute towards the charge of such school:

To the intent therefore that all the encouragement be given to such pious resolutions, and that so necessary and religious an undertaking may be set forward and supported;

Be it enacted by the Governor and Company of the said Colony of Connecticut in General Court Assembled, and it is enacted and ordained by the authority of the same that there be a collegiate school forthwith founded and set up in the town of ——— within this Colony; and that A, B and C, Masters of Arts and Ministers of the Gospel, and E, F, Gentlemen, being all inhabitants within the said Colony be, and hereby are nominated and appointed Trustees for the said School, with full power to contract, agree for, erect, and set up such house, and houseing in ——— aforesaid, as shall be necessary and convenient for the holding and keeping of such school, and to furnish the same for that end; and to employ the money which shall be granted by this Court or otherwise contributed to that use accordingly.

And be it further enacted by the authority aforesaid, that the before named Trustees, together with such others as they shall associate to themselves, so as not to exceed the number of —— in the whole, and their successors to be from time to time nominated by themselves, as any one or more of those first named or associated shall happen to die, be and hereby are further empowered and authorized, from time to time and at all times forever, to have the oversight, direction, rule, order and government of the said school, and provide place and settle a Rector with Tutors and other officers proper and necessary for the teaching, instructing, ruling and governing of the scholars that from time to time shall be sent thither for education, and to make and constitute such rules, orders and laws for that end as are usual and customary in such societies; so as such rules, orders and laws be not repugnant to the laws of the government; as also to confer degrees upon such scholars educated there, who by their good manners and proficiency in learning shall be judged worthy of the same, as is usual and accustomed at Harvard College in Cambridge, within the province of the Massachusetts Bay in New England.

And whereas the principles of the Christian Protestant religion are excellently comprised in the Confession of Faith, composed by the reverend assembly of divines sitting at Westminster, and by the learned and judicious Dr. Ames in his Medulla Theologiæ; the Rector of the same school is to give in charge, and take special care, that the said Book be diligently read in the Latin tongue, and well studied by all scholars educated in the said school.

And it is further enacted by the authority aforesaid, that the said Trustees and their successors be and hereby are further empowered to have, accept, take, acquire and purchase any lands, tenements and hereditaments, to the use of the said school, not exceeding the value of five hundred pounds per annum; and any goods, chattels, sum or sums, of money whatsoever, as from time to time shall be freely given, bequeathed, devised or settled by any person or persons whatsoever upon and to and for the use of the said school, towards the founding, erecting or endowing of the same; and to sue for, recover, and receive all such gifts, legacies, bequests, annuities, rents, issues and profits arising therefrom, and to employ the same accordingly; and out of the estate, revenues, rents, profits and incomes accruing and belonging to the said school to support and pay the Rector, Tutors and other officers their respective annual salaries or allowances.

(6.)

The original Charter of the College.

By the Governor and Council and Representatives of his Majesty's Colony of Connecticut in General Court Assembled, New Haven, Oct. 9th, 1701.

An Act for liberty to erect a Collegiate School.

Whereas, several well-disposed and public spirited persons, of their sincere regard to and zeal for upholding and propagating of the Christian Protestant religion by a succession of learned and orthodox men, have expressed by petition their earnest desires, that full liberty and privilege be granted unto certain undertakers for the founding, suitably endowing and ordering a Collegiate School, within his Majesty's Colony of Connecticut, wherein youth may be instructed in the arts and sciences, who through the blessing of Almighty God may be fitted for public employment both in church and civil state:—to the intent therefore that all due encouragement be given to such pious resolutions, and that so necessary and religious an undertaking may be set forward supported and well managed;

Be it enacted by the Governor and Company of the said Colony of Connecticut in General Court now assembled, and it is enacted and ordained by the authority of the same, that there be and hereby is full liberty, right and privilege granted unto the reverend Mr. James Noyes of Stonington, Mr. Israel Chauncey of Stratford, Mr. Thomas Buckingham of Saybrook, Mr. Abram Pierson of Killingworth, Mr. Samuel Mather of Windsor, Mr. Samuel Andrew of Milford, Mr. Timothy Woodbridge of Hartford, Mr. James Pierpont of New Haven, Mr. Noadiah Russell of Middletown, Mr. Joseph Webb of Fairfield, being reverend ministers of the Gospel, and inhabitants within the said Colony, proposed to stand as Trustees, partners or undertakers for the said School, to them and their successors, to erect, form, direct, order, establish, improve, and at all times, in all suitable ways for the future to encourage the said School in such convenient place or places, and in such form and manner, and under such order and rules as to them shall seem meet and conducive to the aforesaid, and thereof, so as such rules and orders be not repugnant to the laws of the civil government, as also to employ the moneys or any other estate, which shall be granted by this Court or otherwise contributed to that use, according to their discretion, for the benefit of the said Collegiate School, from time to time and at all times henceforward.

And be it farther enacted by the authority aforesaid, that the before named Trustees, Partners, or Undertakers together with such others as they shall associate to themselves, (not exceeding the number of eleven or at any time being less than seven,) provided also that persons nominated or associated from time to time to fill up said number be ministers of the Gospel, inhabiting within this Colony and above the age of forty years,—or the major part of them, the said Mr. James Noyes, Israel Chauncey, Thomas Buckingham, Abram Pierson, Samuel Mather, Samuel Andrew, Timothy Woodbridge, James Pierpont, Noadiah Russell and

Joseph Webb, Undertakers, and of such persons so chosen and associated as above said at any time hereafter,—have and shall have the oversight, full and complete right, liberty, power and privilege to furnish, direct, manage, order, improve and encourage, from time to time and at all times hereafter the said Collegiate School so erected and formed by them in such way, order and manner, and by such person, Rector or Master, and officers appointed by them, as shall, according to their best discretion, be most conducible to attain the aforesaid mentioned end thereof.

And moreover, it is enacted by the Governor, Council and Representatives of the Colony aforesaid met in General Assembly, that the said James Noyes, [etc. as before,] Undertakers, Partners or Trustees, and that said persons taken from time to time into partnership or associated as aforesaid with themselves, shall have and receive,—and it is hereby given and granted unto them,—the full and just sum of one hundred and twenty pounds in country pay, to be paid annually and at all times hereafter, until this Court order otherwise, to them, and to such person or persons only as they shall appoint and empower to receive the same, to be faithfully disposed by the said Trustees, Partners or Undertakers, for the end aforesaid according to their discretion ; which said sum shall be raised and paid in such ways and manners and at such a value, as the country rates of said Colony are and usually have been raised and paid.

And be it further enacted by the authority aforesaid, that the said Undertakers, Partners and their successors be and hereby are further empowered to have, accept, acquire, purchase or otherwise lawfully enter upon any lands, tenements and hereditaments, to the use of said School, not exceeding the value of five hundred pounds per annum, and any goods, chattels, sum or sums of money whatsoever, as have heretofore already been granted, bestowed, bequeathed or given, or as from time to time shall be freely given, bequeathed, devised or settled, by any person or persons whatsoever, upon and to and for the use of the said School, toward the founding, erecting or endowing the same ; and to sue, recover and receive all such gifts, legacies, bequests, annuities, rents, issues and profits arising therefrom, and to employ the same accordingly, and out of the estates, revenues, rents, profits, income, accruing and belonging to the said School, to support and pay, as the said Undertakers shall agree and see cause, the said Rector or Master, Tutors, Ushers or other officers their respective annual salaries or allowances; as also for the encouragement of students to grant degrees or licenses, as they or those deputed by them shall see cause to order and appoint.

(7.)

Remarks on the preceding papers.

From a comparison of these documents it appears—

1. That the unknown author of the 'proposals for erecting an University,' etc., must have been one of the Mathers, (i. e., either Increase, who was deprived of his office as President of Harvard nine days before the date of his letter, or his son Cotton,) or one of their acquaintances. It is clear that this paper was not of Connecticut origin. It speaks of 'inspectors' like Mather's letter and like no other document; it dissuades from erecting a building like Mather and Sewall; and it refers to foreign universities to support this advice as they do.

2. It appears that Mather was not consulted respecting the prospect of a College in the Colony of Connecticut by the leading persons in that project, until a short time before the final action. This could not have been, if a disaffected religious party of which he was a principal member had been forward in this project.

3. It appears that Sewall and Addington were not consulted respecting a draft for a charter until some six weeks or so before the charter was granted, and that certain 'instructions' were transmitted to them what provisions to insert in the draft. The matter has the appearance of one newly brought before their notice, not of one, in which they, as Puritan laymen of the strictest views, had been moving springs.

4. It appears that the actual charter retained a considerable portion of their draft, but dissented most widely from their views in very important particulars.

They represent the collegiate school as founded by the legislature. The ministers to whom the draft was sent draw a pen through these words, and put in their place the words "full liberty for the founding," showing thereby that they mean to have themselves considered as the founders and not the legislature.

They propose to have ministers of the gospel and gentlemen associated as trustees. The Connecticut plan which prevailed was to put affairs in the hands of the ministers alone.

They wish to insert in the charter, and make a great point of it, that the Assembly's Catechism and Ames' Medulla should be studied. In Connecticut it was thought best not to put this into the charter.

Their wish was, although no provision in their charter carries it out, to have a board of visitors. The Connecticut plan was to do without this appendage.

5. It appears that the charter, drawn up by Sewall and Addington, came with a letter dated Oct. 6, while the charter of the College was granted Oct. 9. The letter must have taken two days to reach New Haven. It is plain from this that all the plans of those who were concerned in getting up the new college were laid already ; for otherwise they would not have moved forward with such haste.

6. President Clap says in his history of the College, page 5, that the Assembly in Connecticut "established the act or charter drawn up by the Secretary Addington with some small additions and alterations." But it is plain that he fell into an error, which is a strange one for a man of his accuracy. The Boston Charter was remodelled to secure points which he, of all men, thought vital to the College. This carelessness of President Clap has led President Quincy into the statement that the draft of Sewall and Addington was adopted 'without any material alterations,' and lends some seeming support to his theory respecting the origin of Yale College, which is slenderly supported by historical facts, so far as has yet been ascertained.* And all this has been so fully shown

---

* The following extract of a letter contains the evidence which has been thus far made public. It is from the Rev. Moses Noyes of Lyme, Connecticut, a

by Prof. Kingsley in his review of President Quincy's history of Harvard University that it seems to be placed beyond the reach of doubt.

No. V.

For an early project to establish a College in the Colony of New Haven, started by John Davenport, consult Prof. Kingsley's History of Yale College in the Quarterly Register, vol. 8, p. 14.

The following document copied from the records of Guilford and published by Dr. Dwight in his history of New Haven, must refer to that project.

Trustee of Yale College, dated at Lyme, Sept. 3, 1723, and addressed to Judge Sewall.

"It was an awful stroke of Providence in taking away Mr. Pierpont, in whose assistance I promised myself much benefit to the place, and much ease and comfort to myself, and it is the more afflictive because our young men are feared to be infected with Arminian and Prelatical notions. So that it is difficult to supply his place. It was a wrong step, when the Trustees, by the assistance of great men, removed the College at Saybrook, and a worse, when they put in Mr. Cutler for Rector. The first movers for a College in Connecticut alledged this as a reason, because the College at Cambridge was under the Tutorage of Latitudinarians; but how well they have mended the event sadly manifests. But God is only wise, and will produce glory to his name out of the weaknesses and follies of men."

Mr. Noyes, though not an original Trustee, was living in Connecticut from 1693 onward, and is therefore a good witness. This letter written twenty-five years after the College was projected is proof, certainly, that in the minds of some founders of Yale College, the Tutors at Cambridge were thought latitudinarians and that this was one reason thrown out for founding the new College; but that it was the main or the original reason is not shown by this or any other document, and the absence of all proof, where it could not fail to appear, proves the opposite. President Quincy (vol. ii, 462,) has published a part of the above extract, but has incorrectly given the reading *Tutelage of Latitudinarians* instead of *Tutorage*. Tutelage would refer to the governing board, Tutorage to the instructors at the time; unless Mr. Noyes has used the wrong word: and the difference of the words is plainly an important one, as it respects the bearings of the letter upon the point in question.

"At a General Court, held at Guilford June 28th, A. D. 1652, voted: the matter about a College at New Haven was thought to be too great a charge for us of this jurisdiction to undergo alone; especially considering the unsettled state of New Haven town; being publicly declared from the deliberate judgment of the most understanding men to be a place of no comfortable subsistence for the present inhabitants there. But if Connecticut do join, the planters are generally willing to bear their just proportions for erecting and maintaining of a College there. However they desire thanks to Mr. Goodyear for his kind proffer to the setting forward of such a work."

At the end of the seventeenth century, about 1698, the most forward persons in reviving a project of a College were, according to President Clap, the ministers of New Haven, Milford and Branford, all of them towns of the former New Haven Colony; whence we may conclude that the tradition of the earlier project in the same parts suggested a new and more successful one.

No. VI.

The original sources of information respecting the question of the removal of the College from Saybrook are

1. Johnson's MS. referred to in the text.

2. MSS. in the office of the Secretary of State at Hartford. I have used extracts from these which are supposed to embrace every thing relating to the College. These papers are believed not to have been consulted before.

3. Loose papers in the possession of Yale College.

One of these last papers contains the remonstrance of New London and Hartford counties, and an answer by the Rev. Messrs. Andrew and Russell, two of the Trustees; dated Feb. 22, 1716, (i. e., old style.) In the remonstrance are these words: "and whereas the counties of New London and Hartford being more in numbers than the rest of the government, and paying the greatest part of the money for the subsisting of the Collegiate School, and having furnished the said School with the greatest number of scholars, had reason to expect that in appointing the said School good respect should have been had to them therein, but finding it quite otherwise," etc.

The answer is called, "Some remarks upon the unjust representations, contained in a paper unfairly dispersed through the counties of New London and Hartford, (according to information,) called a remonstrance against the settling of the Collegiate School at New Haven," etc.

One passage of this paper is valuable as containing a distinct reference to the western colonies. "In reference to the number of people, ought they not with the conveniency of the people to have some respect to the flourishing state of the Collegiate School? and is there not a prospect that the western governments, who have no such means of education among them, should contribute more to the advancing the interests of the School than the eastern who are so well furnished at home? Doth the lesser luminary of the heavens ever appear with so great a lustre as when she is farthest from the sun, unless the interposition of the earth eclipse her glory?"

No. VII.

It will be observed that Johnson confines the name Yale College to the building erected for the use of the Collegiate School. Nothing more than this was intended at first. Thus the Trustees say on the records, 'consentimus, statuimus, ordinamus *nostras ædes academicas* patroni munificentissimi nomine appellari atque Yalense Collegium nominari.' And yet for want of a name the *spiritual body*—the Collegiate School—begins to be so called on the records in 1720. The formulæ, 'at a meeting of the Trustees of Yale College,' and 'at a meeting of the Trustees at Yale College' occur interchangeably for several years. Three years afterwards, the act in explanation of and addition to the original Charter, passed Oct. 10, 1723, uses this name as commonly applied to the 'School.' "Whereas, pursuant to the powers and privileges granted to certain Trustees for erecting a Collegiate School in this Colony entitled an act for a Collegiate School, the said Trustees have erected the said School in the town of New Haven, which School is now known by the name of Yale College," etc. President Clap says that "the Trustees, in commendation of Governor Yale's great generosity, called the Collegiate School after his name, Yale College," but he must mean the building by the School. The ambiguity of terms has led many to suppose that the 'Yale College' of 1718 was the same essence as it is now. But it was not until 1745 that by the charter of that year the name covered the body corporate. Meanwhile the building which at first bore the name has disappeared without a vestige.

No. VIII.

Of Rector Cutler, President Stiles speaks in the following terms in his literary diary.

"Rector Cutler was an excellent linguist—he was a great Hebrician and Orientalist. He had more knowledge of the Arabic than I believe any man before him except President Chauncey and his disciple the first Mr. Thatcher. Dr. Cutler was a good Logician, Geographer and Rhetorician. He spoke Latin with fluency and dignity and with great propriety of pronunciation. He was a noble Latin orator, as I learn from my father, who was educated under him. From him and Rev. Mr. Edwards of Windsor, my father an excellent Latinist learned to pronounce Latin; and I from my father, who often called me when a boy, to hear him read Latin like Dr. Cutler. He was of a commanding presence and dignity in government. He was a man of extensive reading in the academic sciences, divinity and ecclesiastical history. He was of a high, lofty and despotic mien. He made a grand figure as the head of a College. But his head being at length turned with the splendor of prelacy, and carried away with the fond enterprize of Episcopizing all New England, he, in 1722, turned Churchman, left his Rectorate of Yale College, and was reordained by the Bishop of

Norwich, and was honored with the Doctorate in Divinity from Oxford and Cambridge. Returning he settled in Boston; but failed of that influence and eminence which he figured to himself in prospect."

The Rev. Ernest Hawkins, Secretary of the Society for the propagation of the Gospel, whose missionary Dr. Cutler was, in his "historical notices of missions of the Church of England," gives a fair account of this movement of Dr. Cutler and others towards Episcopacy, as well as extracts from their letter. For the claim of Dr. Cutler, when settled in Boston, to a seat in the Board of Overseers of Harvard College, see President Quincy's History, Chap. XVII.

According to Hollis, (Quincy, u. s.) Dr. Cutler said to him, "I was never in judgment heartily with the Dissenters, but bore it patiently until a favorable opportunity offered. This has opened at Boston, and I now declare publicly what I before believed privately." This as Hollis reports it looks like dishonest dissimulation; but perhaps Dr. Cutler meant no more than that for a time there was a struggle between his religious convictions and his prospects.

No. IX.

President Stiles in his diary has recorded the following information respecting the interregnum of 1722–26.

"Mr. John Whiting of Windham, Aet. 70 et supra, graduated at Yale College in 1726: this journey I saw him, when he gave me the following account of the monthly Rectors, when he first entered College in 1722. Though all agreed to take their turns, yet six of the Trustees only actually came and resided at New Haven, viz., Rev. Mr. Woodbridge, Mr. Russell, Mr. Davenport, Mr. Andrew, Mr. Buckingham of Hartford, and Mr. Whitman: neither Mr. Adams nor the rest came. Mr. Woodbridge moderated at Commencement, 1723, Mr. Andrew, 1724, and [was] then elected stated Rector pro tempore till another should be chosen; and he served three years, and was considered, called, and treated as standing Rector.

No. X.

Of that versatile and sagacious man, Rector Williams, President Stiles, in his diary, gives the following account, under the title of 'Memoirs of the Rev. Rector Williams.'

"A.D. 1694. Aug. 24. Born at Hatfield, son of Rev. William Williams.

1708. Admitted Sophimore in Harvard College, and educated under Mr. Tutor Remington.

1711. } Graduated A.B. and A.M. by Mr. President Lev-
1714. } erett; and soon married Miss Eunice Chester, and settled at Wethersfield.

1717. Made Tutor of refugee scholars at Wethersfield by the Rev. Messrs. Woodbridge and Buckingham, two Trustees; afterwards chosen and approved at a legal meeting of the Trustees of College.

1718. Member and Clerk of the Assembly.

1720. Severe fit of sickness—sanctified.

1721. Æ. 27. Ordained Pastor of the Church in Newington.

1726. Æ. 33. Installed Rector of Yale College. Elected 1725. He filled his chair with great usefulness and honor thirteen years.

1739. Æ. 46. He resigned the Rectorate and was succeeded by Mr. Clap. He removed to Wethersfield; was elected member of the General Assembly; constituted Judge of the Superior Court.

1745. Æ. 51. Went Chaplain of the Army in Cape Breton expedition.

1746. Became Colonel of a regiment in the proposed Canada expedition.

1750. (?) Went to England—became acquainted with the Rev. Dr. Doddridge, and married Mrs. Scott of Norwich.

1752. Apr. 24. Returned to New England, and lived a merchant.

1755. July 24. Died at Wethersfield, Æ. 61."

In another place, President Stiles writes thus: "Mr. Rector Williams was a good classical scholar, well versed in Logic Metaphysics and Ethics, and in Rhetoric and Oratory. He presided at Commencement with great honor. He spoke Latin freely, and delivered orations gracefully and with animated dignity. While a boy, I heard him make his valedictory oration at the Commencement, 1739, when he resigned his office. He was a man of splendor!"

No. XI.

David Brainerd was expelled in the winter of 1742, because he refused to make a public confession,—then a very common thing,—for certain words dropped in private conversation derogatory to the religious character of Mr. Whittelsey, a Tutor; and also because he had disobeyed College law by going to a 'separate' meeting; as well as on account of another charge, which was not admitted by him and probably not much relied upon. See for this affair the lives of him, Edwards' in Dwight's edition of his works, vol. 10, and Peabody's in Sparks' biography. Peabody errs in saying that Whittelsey showed himself to be what Brainerd denounced him. This is an unintentional injury done to the character of a sincerely good man. Brainerd might have been restored again to his College standing in 1743, on condition of residence, but being old and already engaged in missionary labors he declined so doing. This treatment of Brainerd was in conformity with a law passed in 1741, to the effect that if any student should denounce any of the College authorities as being 'hypocrites carnal or unconverted men;' he should for the first offence be required to make public confession, and for the second be expelled.

Brainerd was over one and twenty when he entered College, and possibly he fared the worse on account of his mature age. In 1744, a law was passed, which may have been suggested by this case, that no person should be admitted a Freshman who was more than twenty-one years old.

The case of the two Cleavelands may be found fully detailed in the eighth chapter of Dr. Trumbull's second volume. It came up in Nov., 1744, and for final action in Jan., 1745, and exhibited more intolerance than the dealings with Brainerd. These two persons however subsequently received degrees.

That these proceedings were censurable, both on the score of severity and of disregard of conscientious convictions, probably all will admit: it should be remembered however that they were of a piece with much of the conduct of the principal persons of the Colony at this time. Those of the clergy of Connecticut, whose attachment to Calvinism was lukewarm or doubtful, who incurred the reproach with more or less justice of being 'Arminians,' together with the leading persons in civil life, were united in bitter opposition to the Separatists, and the more zealous promoters of the religious movements in the year 1740, and afterward. Thus in the Associations of ministers in this Colony, Whitfield's conduct and that of his followers was unsparingly censured. The legislature also, in 1742, passed an intolerant law against itinerating ministers, and the ecclesiastical laws of the Colony were brought to bear heavily upon Separatists from the Congregational churches, although at this time Baptists and Episcopalians enjoyed toleration.

In the year 1742, at the same session in May to which we referred just above, a committee was appointed by the legislature to take into consideration 'that paragraph of his Honor's speech, made to [the] assembly, relating to the unhappy circumstances of the College.' To the report of this committee on the State records eight names are appended, one of which seems to be that of ex-rector Williams, and two others those of graduates of the College. The committee say that by enquiry they have ascertained that "some of the students have fallen into the practice of rash judging and censuring others, even some of the governors, teachers and instructors of the College, as being unconverted, unexperienced and unskillful guides in matters of religion, and have therefore contemptuously refused to submit to their authority;" etc., that "some undergraduate students have made it their practice day and night, and sometimes for several days together, to go about in the town of New Haven, as well as in other towns, and before great numbers of people to teach and exhort, much after the same manner that ministers of the Gospel do in their public preaching;" that "pains have been taken to prejudice the minds of students against our ecclesiastical constitution, and to persuade them to attend on private and separate meetings, and that sundry of the students have so done in contempt of the laws and authority of the College;" and that these things "have been a hindrance to the flourishing of religion and vital piety in that society, and if tolerated may defeat the good ends and designs of that institution." The committee therefore advise that the instructors of the College "be very careful to instruct the students in the true principles of religion according to our Confession of Faith and ecclesiastical constitution, and to keep them from all such errors as they may be in danger of imbibing from strangers and foreigners; [i. e., itinerant ministers,] and to use all such proper measures as are in their power, to prevent their being under the influence and instruction of such, as would prejudice their minds against the way of worship and ministry established by the laws of this government; and that order and authority be duly maintained in that society, and that those should not enjoy the privileges of it who contumaciously refuse to submit to the laws, orders and rules thereof, which have been made or shall be made according to the powers and instructions given in their charter: but we think it highly reasonable," they say, "that all proper means be first used with such scholars, that they may be reclaimed and reduced to order before they be dismissed as incorrigible." They then add that, as there was a project of requesting certain "experienced grave divines" to repair to New Haven to instruct the scholars by their sermons, the Assembly be recommended to grant the Trustees a sum of money to pay for the supply of the pulpits of such divines when absent from home on such an errand.

This report was concurred in and accepted by both houses; and virtually lent their approbation to the course taken with David Brainerd a little before. Governor Law, who called the subject up in his speech before the Assembly, strongly disapproved of the religious movement; and may have intended to throw the shield of the legislature's protection over the authorities of the College.

The two Cleavelands sent in a memorial to the General Assembly in 1745, at the May session, praying for a redress of their grievances and to be immediately restored to their standing in College. In a well written document they recite the reasons for their father's separating, with a majority of the church members, from the religious society in Canterbury ; and complain that they had been punished for that which was not against College law. They make the whole question turn upon the respective rights of the church and congregation in choosing a minister ; that being the point on which a majority of the church had separated from a majority of the congregation in this instance. They say near the close of their petition, and with reason as people now think ; " may it please your Honors, as we understand the laws of this Colony, the Congregational persuasion is as much under the countenance of the laws of this Colony as the Saybrook platformists are ; and therefore we think it hard measure indeed to be cut off from our College privileges, merely for being of the Congregational persuasion, and acting agreeable thereto, while the Saybrook platformists, professors of the Church of England, Seven day and [other] Baptists and Quakers have and have had free liberty to enjoy all the privileges of College, their principles and practices in the vacancies of College agreeable thereto notwithstanding."

This petition produced no effect, but was dismissed in both houses.

The exciting cause of the intolerance at this period lay, as is apparent from what has preceded, in the wild fanaticism of Davenport and others, who denounced ministers and others by name as unconverted men and hypocrites, broke up congregations, and sowed the seeds of discord in parishes. I suppose that the same excesses, occurring again, though not met by legal penalties, would be punished in some other more disorderly way. I figure to myself how another Davenport would fare, if he should start upon a crusade through the southern states denouncing slaveholders and slaveholding ministers as hypocrites and unconverted men. Does any body suppose, that if he crossed Mason and Dixon's line whole, he would reach Charleston whole ?

It is amusing to perceive how those, who had the least to do with the transient excesses of those times in New England, were annoyed by them. Dr. Cutler writes to the society for the propagation of the Gospel in 1741 as follows: "I need only mention one [follower of Whitfield] Gilbert Tennent, a teacher living to the southward, who visited us the last winter and afflicted us more than the most intense cold and snow that was ever known among us, and kept even the most tender people travelling night and day, to hear the most vulgar crude and boisterous things from him, to the ruin of the health of many and the poisoning of more with unsound divinity; so that charity is much extinguished, order violated, visionaries young and old abound, and think themselves obliged to exhibit their gifts of praying and expounding to all that will attend them," etc. If they, through whose fields the wildfire had the least spread, by a natural love of order and antipathy to overwarmth were led to speak in strong terms of censure against the revivalists of 1740, how much less was it to be expected that those Congregational ministers should keep calm, who were stung continually by charges of being carnal, lukewarm, and hypocrites. By such invectives, forgetful of the meek spirit of their master, they were goaded into intolerance.

But—to close where I began with Brainerd,—I cannot forbear quoting a passage from the Rev. Dr. Bacon's excellent Historical Discourses, in which he deals justice to that man of God and to the Tutor whom he insulted. After citing some passages from a fragment of Mr. Whittelsey's private journal, the author proceeds as follows, p. 248:

"I might say now, if I supposed that there were any doubt here respecting the piety of this man, Compare these breathings of penitence and devotion with any parallel passages in Brainerd's own journal, and tell me whether even Brainerd's records seem more like the broken heart and the contrite spirit which God will not despise, or more like the heart that knows its own deceitfulness. But I choose rather to call your attention to another view. Brainerd, who always felt whatever he did feel with all his soul, and who knew as little as a child, of the analysis of complicated motives and emotions,—Brainerd, carried away with a gust of inconsiderate zeal and a spirit of censoriousness caught by his quick sympathy with others, and admitting the passionate extravagances of the wandering Davenport, saw nothing which seemed to him like the grace of God, in the staid, self-possessed, decorous piety of Tutor Whittelsey. To him, the Tutor's prayers against self-deception, and for a knowledge of the deceitfulness of the heart, however fervent and pathetic, however full of humiliation and contrition, seemed formal and dead, compared with the freedom and fearlessness, the familiarity and vulgarity of the itinerants, whose preaching caused so great an excitement. The Rector and Tutors, on the other hand, were very naturally dissatisfied with that sort of piety, which was inconsistent not only with what they esteemed decorum, but with the order of College, and with a due attention to the daily duty of study. They were alarmed at the growing propensity among the students to violate not only the rules of College, but the law of the land, by running away from the appointed place of worship to the separate meeting. They probably had an eye on Brainerd, as one who would be likely by his religious zeal to come into conflict with their authority. And very likely they were quite willing to be rid of him, and to inflict a signal blow upon the intemperate spirit of the times, by dealing sternly with him for that calumnious censure of his superior. Accordingly, Brainerd was disgraced and expelled; and though he afterwards made ample and penitent confession of all that was wrong in his conduct on that occasion, he could not be restored. They doubtless had as low an idea of his piety, as he, in his most censorious mood had of theirs. Their common error had a common cause. They judged of each other by a wrong standard. They yielded to their feelings, their party prejudices, their antipathies. Brainerd was a child of God, though he was carried away by the unhappy extravagancies of the times:—even then the processes were going on within him, by which the Spirit of God made him afterwards, so illustrious an example of holiness. He too, whom Brainerd pronounced graceless, was a child of God, notwithstanding his opposition to what Brainerd deemed the work of God:—even then he was keeping his heart with all diligence, and struggling to bring every thought into subjection to the Gospel."

No. XII.

I place in this appendix some documents showing how President Clap was estimated by his College contemporaries and acquaintances.

Extract of a letter from President Daggett to Dr. Stiles, dated Feb. 28, 1769.

Agreeable to your request, which will ever be a law to me, I here send you a copy of President Clap's oration [on resigning his office,] taken from the College records, in which you will view the image of that great good man, your instructor and mine; not perhaps without some little inaccuracies of composition and inelegance of Latin style. But with these very little defects I scarcely know of any possession at my dispose, which I would not freely give up, to be made possessor of that large rich fund of useful learning, which he had acquired.

Extract of a letter from Dr. Stiles to Prof. Daggett, dated Newport, July 28, 1767.

In your favor of the 15th inst., you ask an extract from a letter in which I made some strictures upon President Clap, to join with your sermon at his funeral. I thought it would better answer your view to draw his character according to my idea of it than to detach a few extracts from a hasty epistle. This I have done partly by extracting from that letter, and partly from my present recollection. Though I honor the memory of my once Macaenas, yet I have not the same idea and opinion of the wisdom of his conduct, as I have of his learning,—and therefore have confined myself entirely to his literary character. Different judgments are formed of him,—this is mine.

Some passages from his 'strictures.'

The reverend President Clap was possessed of strong rational powers, clear perception and solid judgment. Though not eminent for learning yet he had a competent knowledge of the three learned languages. In mathematics and natural philosophy I have not reason to think that he was equalled by any man in America, except by the only man by whom he was surpassed,—the most learned Professor Winthrop.—Wollaston's religion of nature was the basis of his moral philosophy, and he understood it well. The former part of his own treatise on ethics is founded in sublime truth.—Westminster Calvinism was his theology ; and he was a perfect master of it.—I think he was rather a supra than a sub-lapsarian, and the doctrine of the decrees in the most absolute sense was the basis of all his ideas of God's moral government. He had with great attention studied the Scriptures upon the doctrines of original sin, the divinity and satisfaction of Christ, justification by the imputation of his righteousness, and irresistible grace in conversion. In these doctrines he conceived the essence of religion to consist.—All other doctrines he held to be of a subordinate nature and examined them with much less attention. But on these fundamental doctrines he had read the most eminent divines of the last two hundred years : and in his peculiar manner, very much passing over other subjects in their writings, he had examined so many authors through the tract from Jerome to the present day as well as the three primitive ages, that on these subjects I believe him to have been possessed of the sentiments of the whole Christian world, especially when they agreed with his own. But in polemical divinity he failed, and it is doubted, whether he had the happiest talent at conceiving and presenting the sentiments, principles and views of Arminians, Arians and deists.—History, ancient and modern, political and ecclesiastical, he was well versed in : he was, I judge, far more copiously read in philosophy and history than in divinity, which last, however, he was fond of conceiving as his favorite study.—Herodotus, Diodorus Siculus and the summary compends of the Roman history, as Eutropius, Velleius Paterculus and others, he read thoroughly. Livy, Dionysius and the other voluminous historians he only turned to for illustration of momentous events.—If any should think that I exhibit too high an idea of [his] knowledge of history, I have only to say that during the whole thirteen years of my residence at Yale College, I was most intimately acquainted with his manner of study and the subjects of his researches: and this at the period of life, when he prosecuted them with the greatest vigor and formed his final judgment upon them. He read much in Strype and Burnet, and I think Quick's Synodicon was a favorite author with him.—He greatly studied the councils general and particular, and in them, I believe, was more thoroughly versed than any man in America. Hardouin's voluminous Collection employed many of his reading hours. The councils, fathers and rabbinical writings were read by the ministers that first settled New England much beyond what they have been by their successors. President Clap had no acquaintance with the rabbinical writings worthy the title of knowledge; but in the fathers and councils I do not think he was excelled by many of the New England fathers besides Hooker and Norton.—He was considerably read in the Common law of England.—With such abundant furniture it is surprising that he should figure no more as a writer. His 'ethics' is his best piece of composition: his 'history of Yale College' will survive the oblivion of several other pieces, more as a collection of important memoirs than for the manner in which they are digested. He wrote a piece on the theory of comets and another on the grounds of music, which, if they were printed, would honor him as a mathematician.—The labors of his office left but few hours for reading, nor was he after all a great reader. But he was possessed of a happy and advantageous method of reading:—he seldom read a volume through in course: having previously settled in his mind the particular subjects he would examine, he then pitched directly on those books which would elucidate the subject of his enquiry. He would thus with great assiduity, discernment and dispatch turn over and examine fifty volumes, if necessary, and select whatever they contained in point; and thus proceed till he had made himself master of the subject, passing unconcerned over the rest of the book, and generally uncaught by any other matter, however attracting and interesting."

In his literary diary, President Stiles thus expresses himself of President Clap.

"Mr. Clap, though no classical scholar, was however of a stronger mind than Mr. Williams, and surpassed him as well as all the Presidents in Harvard College, and in all American colleges in

Mathematics, Natural Philosophy and Astronomy. His reasoning powers were good and well improved. He had a singular talent with little reading of gaining great knowledge, and became at length acquainted with almost every subject in the whole circle of literature. Had he been possessed of politeness, [i. e., of acquaintance with polite literature,] he would have figured as one of the lights, one of the first literary characters of the age. He was not boisterous or noisy, but still, quiet, contemplative, resolute, firm, immovable even to absolute despotism: not properly haughty, but *sic volo sic jubeo* was inwrought in his make. This rendered the latter part of his Presidency uncomfortable. He was indefatigable in labors both secular and scientific for the good of the College; the one in building a new College edifice and chapel of brick; the other in frequent public dissertations upon all kinds of literature. As to his person he was not tall, yet being thick set he appeared rather large and bulky."

Dr. Dwight in his statistical account of New Haven, published by the Connecticut Academy in 1807, speaks in the following terms of President Clap. "His character is extensively given in a manner highly honorable to him in an appendix to the life of President Stiles from a diary of that gentleman by the Rev. Dr. Holmes of Cambridge.* To him who reads this character there will remain little doubt that he was the greatest man who ever sat at the head of the Institution."

"Mr. Richard Woodhull, who was five years [*read* two years] a Tutor under his administration, and was himself universally distinguished for learning and science, once gave me the following character of President Clap in answer to some inquiries which I made concerning this subject. If I were to give his character in College terms—said Mr. Woodhull,—I should give it in this manner: In whatever company he was, and whatever was the subject of conversation he appeared evidently to understand it more clearly and more comprehensively than any other person. As

---

* Dr. Dwight makes a trifling error here. The four last lines in Dr. Holmes' appendix relating to President Clap are from Stiles' diary; the rest from the letter from which I had made extracts before knowing that Dr. Holmes had done the same.

Mr. Woodhull had not long before a controversy with President Clap, he cannot be supposed to be prejudiced in his favor. The only serious defect in his presidential character was that he was prone to consider boys as being men."

No. XIII.

President Stiles has the following account of Dr. Daggett in his diary.

"He was born at Attleborough, Sept. 8, 1727. Rev. Solomon Reed took him and Foster and Cobb of that vicinity, in 1743, as charity scholars to educate liberally for the ministry. Mr. Reed, then a candidate for the ministry, brought them with him from Middleborough to Canterbury or Plainfield in Connecticut, where Rev. Mr. Cogswell was keeping school. Mr. Daggett was here about half a year under the faithful grammar instruction of Mr. Cogswell. This was the main classical instruction he ever received. Removing from Plainfield to Abington in Massachusetts with Mr. Reed, he there studied the New Testament to Revelations. At the end of the vacancy, 1744, Mr. Reed carried his three pupils, one of whom [was] Mr. Daggett, to enter into Harvard College. But the last day was nearly past, and it was said Mr. Reed had brought three new light scholars: so they were refused without examination, the time being said to be elapsed. Upon this Mr. Reed brought Daggett and Cobb to Yale College in the fall. Before this however the Rev. Mr. Welde of Attleborough, resenting the matter himself, carried Daggett, etc., again to Cambridge, and remonstrated to the President with great severity, but they still refused. Upon which Mr. Reed brought them to New Haven, that is Cobb and Daggett, leaving Foster behind. Daggett and Cobb were admitted 1744 at Yale College. Cobb turned out a profligate. Daggett studied well and graduated 1748. About 1751 he was settled and ordained at Smithtown, L. I., and 1755 was chosen Professor of Divinity in Yale College, and was installed 1756. In 1766, he was made President pro tempore, which he resigned 1777."

Dr. Dwight, who was both a student and an officer of Yale College under President Daggett, thus speaks of him, in his statistical account of New Haven, p. 71.

"Dr. Daggett was respectable as a scholar, a divine and a preacher. He had very just conceptions of the manner in which a College should be governed, but was not always happy in the mode of administering its discipline. A number of persons were not willing to do justice to his merits. I say this with confidence, because I was acquainted with him for a long time in the most intimate manner. The College was eminently prosperous under his Presidency. His sermons were judicious, clear, solemn, and impressive."

No. XIV.

As two extensive biographies of President Stiles have appeared, one by his son-in-law, the Rev. Dr. Holmes of Cambridge, Mass., and the other by Prof. Kingsley, in Sparks' Collection of American Biographies, it would be idle to say any thing in this place respecting his life or the estimate in which he was held by his contemporaries. May I be permitted to quote two passages from his diary, the first showing the amount of his academical labors, and the second his private feelings in view of those labors.

"The business of the Professorship of Divinity now devolves on me for the present, and besides my history lecture, I weekly give a public dissertation on astronomical subjects, besides my private or chamber lecture on theology every Saturday afternoon. And besides these I attend every day the recitations of the Senior and Junior classes in philosophy, i. e., each, one recitation a day. So that I am called to fill the offices of three professorships and the Presidency at the same time. And yet the Corporation keep me in so poor and parsimonious a manner that domestic cares and the *res angustæ domi* are a heavier anxiety to me than all my College cares."—*Stiles' Diary under the date of Nov.* 28, 1780, *just after the death of Dr. Daggett, Professor of Divinity.*

Dec. 10, 1780, he writes,

"Through the long suffering and patience of God I am this day fifty-three years old, three months younger than Dr. Daggett. Every year gives new experience of the divine care and goodness. Now that I am growing old the greatest cares are devolved upon me; not only those of the Presidency and professorship of Ecclesiastical History, but for the present the superadded ones of the Professorship of Divinity. I have great need of the grace of Jesus. Who is sufficient for these things? The good Lord make his grace sufficient, his grace and strength perfect through my weakness. I would begin this year with God and commit myself to his holy keeping."

No. XV.

Stiles' Diary, July 8, 1778.

"The oath of fidelity administered to me by the Hon. Col. Hamlin, one of the Council of the State of Connecticut, at my inauguration.

"You, Ezra Stiles, do swear by the name of the ever-living God that you will be true and faithful to the State of Connecticut, as a free and independent State, and in all things do your duty as a good and faithful subject of the said State, in supporting the rights liberties and privileges of the same. So help you God.

"This oath substituted instead of that of allegiance to the king by the Assembly of Connecticut, May, 1777, to be taken by all in this State: and so it comes into use in Yale College."

No. XVI.

Changes in the nature and relations of College officers have by degrees altered the type of American colleges. The first academical corps consisted of a Rector or President and a number of

Tutors, all designed to be permanent. Such was the Faculty of Harvard at its foundation. Next we find a President and a number of Tutors who filled their places but a short time. Next came in the professorial element, which, gaining strength by degrees, has now a predominance in nearly all colleges. This introduction of a permanent body of men, having charge of the several departments or sciences and of mature age, has altered the old system from a *monarchy* or something like it, in which the President had a controlling power, into a polity where the officers are equal. The present system may hereafter feel the effects of change also. Either a corps of Tutors may be abolished on the one hand, or a permanent President may be found unnecessary on the other. The first change I should dread, for it is not safe to leave a College exclusively in the hands of elderly or even of middle aged men. They are in danger of becoming tired of instructing particularly in the elements; and cannot always understand the wants of a new age. An element of youthful vigor, mingled up with this permanent one, seems necessary for the best interests of colleges; but in my judgment the best way of doing this has not yet been tried: it is to have a body of Fellows, or graduated scholars, elected according to merit, and devoted by the tenure of their office to the study of science and learning, from among whom the Tutors might be chosen. The substitution of a temporary for a permanent President I anticipate as likely to be viewed with favor by the next generation.

No. XVII.

From President Stiles' Diary, Nov. 9, 1779.

" Books recited by the several classes at my accession to the Presidency.

Freshman Class.—Virgilius, Ciceronis orationes, Græc. Test., Ward's Arithmetic.

Sophimore Class.*—Græcum Testament., Horatius, Lowth's English Grammar, Watts' Logic, Guthrie's Geography, Hammond's Algebra, Holmes' Rhetorick, Ward's Geometry, Vincent's Catechism, [Saturday] Ward's Mathematics.

Junior Class.—Ward's Trigonometry, Atkinson and Wilson do., Græc. Test., Cicero de Oratore, Martin's Philosophic Grammar and Philosophy, 3 vols., Vincent, [Saturday].

Senior Class.—Locke, human understanding, Wollaston, relig. nature delineated, and for [Saturday] Wollebius, Amesii Medulla, Græc. Test., (or Edwards on the Will, sometime discontinued,) President Clap's Ethics."

And again, 1778, July 27, just after his accession, he writes:

"I this day began to instruct a class in Hebrew and the oriental languages, which I selected out of all the other classes, as they voluntarily offered themselves. This is not required of a President, but I wish to benefit them to the utmost of my power. Johnson is the only undergraduate that now understands anything of Hebrew; he has read something in the Psalter. Mr. Tutor Baldwin is a good Hebrician. The other Tutors and Professors have some small knowledge of it. It has always been usual to initiate every class a little into it, but the dispersed state of the scholars for two years past has prevented this and other usual studies."

And again, June 24, 1779:

"Yesterday I put the Senior Class into President Clap's Ethics, or Moral Philosophy. It was printed just before his death, and has been sometimes recited by the classes. Afterwards President Edwards on the will was recited: this giving offence was dropt. And through the confusion of the times the Seniors have recited no ethics for several years. When I was [an] undergraduate [1742–46] we recited Wollaston's religion of nature delineated. When my father was in College [1722] they recited Mori enchiridion ethicum."

---

* For this, the original way of spelling this word, and for the word itself see Dr. Goodrich's remarks (s. v.) in his edition of Webster's Dictionary.

No. XVIII.

Silas Deane, on his return from France, was desirous to have the modern languages studied at this College, and accordingly wrote to President Stiles not long after his accession to that effect. After mentioning the neglect of such studies at places of public education here and in Europe, and their importance, particularly to men doing public business like himself, he adds: "I therefore take the liberty to propose,—should it be agreeable to you and the reverend Corporation to patronize the design,—soliciting assistance from some of my noble aad opulent friends in France, to establish a Professor of the French language in your College, and to make a collection of the writings of their most celebrated authors for your library. I have repeatedly mentioned the proposal in general to many of them at Paris, and have no doubt it may be carried into execution."

His plan was much talked of, and met with the approbation of most persons whom President Stiles consulted; but was never carried into execution, owing perhaps in part to the undeserved disgrace into which Deane fell.

No. XIX.

It may not be uninteresting to those for whom especially this discourse was written, if I add here some accounts of the July examination day and quarter days, as they were seventy years ago from Stiles' diary, July 23, 1778. Nothing could place in stronger contrast the importance attached to academical forms at that day and neglect of them at present. "This day—was attended the public examination of the Senior Class. The examinators sent the Junior Tutor and Vice-Bedellus to wait upon the President in the library, to ask leave and authority to examine, etc. The President granted leave, and delivered them a Diploma, empowering the Professors, Tutors and graduates, etc. This being read in the Chapel, the Senior Tutor presiding in the examination, the consessus examinatorius proceeded and examined the candidates in the languages, particularly in Cicero de Oratore, and the Greek Testament. A recess of half an hour. Then resuming the exercise, the examination proceeded through the circle of the sciences. The Professor of Divinity, two ministers of the town and another minister having accompanied me to the library about 1 P. M., the middle Tutor waited upon me there, and informed that the examination was finished and they were ready for the presentation. I gave leave, being seated in the library between the above ministers. Hereupon the examiners, preceded by the Professor of Mathematics, entered the library, and introduced thirty candidates,—a beautiful sight! The diploma examinatorium with the return and minutes inscribed upon it, was delivered to the President, who gave it to the Vice-bedellus, directing him to read it. He read it and returned it to the President, to be deposited among the College archives in perpetuam rei memoriam. The Senior Tutor thereupon made a very eloquent Latin speech, and presented the candidates for the honors of the College. This presentation the President in a Latin speech accepted, and addressed the gentlemen examiners and the candidates, and gave the latter liberty to return home till Commencement. Then dismissed.

At about 3 P. M. the afternoon exercises were appointed to begin. At 3½ the bell tolled, and the assembly convened in the chapel, ladies and gentlemen. The President introduced the exercises in a Latin speech, and then delivered the diploma examinatorium to the Vice-bedellus, who, standing on the pulpit stairs, read it publicly. Then succeeded

Cliosophic Oration in Latin, by Sir Meigs.

Poetical Composition in English, by Sir Barlow.

Dialogue, English, by { Sir Miller.
Sir Chaplin.
Sir Ely.

Cliosophic Oration, English, by Sir Webster.

Disputation, English, by { Sir Wolcott.
Sir Swift.
Sir Smith.

Valedictory Oration, English, by Sir Tracy.

An Anthem. Exercises two hours."

[It was the fashion then to call a Bachelor of Arts Sir, and this is here done at the time when the Seniors were accepted for that degree. Bachelors were called senior, middle or junior Bachelors according to the year since graduation and before taking the degree of master. Nearly all these persons attained to some distinction in after life. Meigs was Professor of mathematics in the College, Barlow the well known poet and embassador to France, Miller and Swift, Judges of the Supreme Court of Connecticut, the latter the writer on law, Smith, a Judge in Vermont, Wolcott, Secretary of the Treasury of the United States, Webster, the Lexicographer, Tracy, Senator of the United States.]

No. XX.

This seems to be not an inappropriate place to say a few words respecting the financial state of the College, its wants, and the enlargement at which it ought to aim. May I not hope that fifty years hence, if an address like this shall be delivered, there will be no occasion for a similar representation.

In 1830, Yale College seemed to be approaching bankruptcy. In consequence of the statements of its condition then made, its graduates and other friends contributed $100,000, of which about 89,000 were appropriated to the general funds of the College proper or academical department, with which alone I am concerned at this time. Since that time the fund of the Clark professorship has reached the amount prescribed by the donor, viz., $20,000, and Mr. Munson has left a bequest of $15,000 to the College. Besides these, smaller amounts have been given for specific purposes, such as the library, and scholarships, and another of $4,000, being chargeable with an annuity, yields a very trifling income.

The funds now possessed by the College appropriated by their donors to specific objects other than the endowment of professorships and not capable of being used for the support of the academical corps, amount to about $80,000.

The general funds, and funds for the support of Professors amount to about $140,000.

The average income from these last named funds and from term bills is from funds, $10,000, and somewhat over; from tuition fees of Students $11,000, or somewhat under, that is $21,000 with a net amount from room rent, which will not greatly vary from $2,000.

The expenses of the College for the salaries of a President, nine Professors, six Tutors, a Treasurer, a Librarian, an assistant in chemistry, lecturers in law and anatomy, and a teacher in elocution amount to nearly $19,000; leaving $4000 for the numberless incidental expenses of a great literary Institution, such as apparatus, laboratory expenses, expenses for Commencements, Corporation meetings, repairs of public buildings not compensated by term bills, etc. The treasury has been so well managed that for a number of years there has been a small annual surplus, excepting when a public building was erected or underwent extensive repairs. But this end has been secured by paying extremely small salaries to the officers. The Professors receive less than $1150, a sum which is entirely inadequate to maintain a family with respectability in New Haven. And this salary remains almost exactly as it was fixed thirty three years since.

It is obvious then that the receipts of the College are only sufficient with rigid economy in ordinary times, and with the present large number of students, to keep it on its present course; but that they would be unequal to any enlargement of any kind, whether new College buildings should be needed, or new instruction, or the cabinet or apparatus should require additions. It is obvious also that if the number of students should be materially diminished, the principal of the funds would need to be drawn upon for necessary annual expenses, as was the case before 1830.

There is one way of increasing the means of the College which will readily suggest itself to every one: I refer to an increase in the tuition, which is now very small, viz., $33 per annum. This has been often thought of; but there are reasons against it lying not so much in the interests of the College, as in the higher interests of public education. Suppose for instance the tuition fees were doubled, and that this would deter half the number of students from applying for admission, which is probably far too large an amount of effect to be assigned to the cause: even then with the same receipts the number of instructors might be lessened and the Institution would be a gainer in its funds. But when we consider at what an expense to public interests this would be effected, that the children of the poor and of persons in moderate circumstances would be deprived of education,—a class from which the best scholars and the most valuable members of society in after life are apt to come,—and that the College, let the officers do what they would, could scarcely fail of degenerating in scholarship and orderliness through the absence of this class of students; we can hardly, as well wishers to our country and to the cause of public intelligence, consent to such a method of securing a good to the College by means of a great public evil. We are not prepared to believe indeed that gratuitous education will be good education in the general; but on the other hand the means of sending a son to College and of carrying him through College ought to be within the reach of all who can with some self-denial effect it. And this is the view of collegiate education which has been taken by enlightened persons both in England and among ourselves; that it is not properly to be self-supporting, but that, as well by funds invested without return for the general benefit, as by special helps such as scholarships, the burdens of education are to be lessened. Let any one look at the *exhibitions* and other aids to students at the English Universities, and notice how many of the greatest and best men, whether churchmen or men of letters, have been enabled by them to secure an education; and he will not think lightly of the benefit which the piety of past ages has in this way perpetuated in England. In this country perhaps none of the older colleges, if any college at all, receives back income from half the funds which it has spent for the benefit of students and which are actually yielding a benefit. The calculation has been made at Yale College, that if the students were to pay the interest at six per cent. of all the moneys spent in libraries, cabinets, public buildings and other fixtures intended for their use; tuition would be threefold greater than it now is. No public institution could live on a different principle.

It will probably be admitted then by all, unless indeed those who judge of this subject exclusively on the principles of political economy be an exception, that colleges ought not to be self-supporting institutions; and that Yale College ought to look for its means of advancement not to an increase in the price of tuition, but to the liberality of its graduates and other friends. That it has maintained the high standing in public esteem, which has been conceded to it for the last half century, is owing principally to the generosity of the State in 1792, and to that of private contributors in 1830. But it might also be shown, if it were proper to speak of such a thing in its details, that self-denying efforts and subscriptions on the part of its officers have conduced in a considerable measure to the material prosperity of the College, or I should rather say, to its relief from severe embarrassments.

In looking at the future and asking what ought to be the progress of the College hereafter, so many objects important to be attained rise before my mind that I hardly dare enumerate them. It requires some boldness to tell a story of great wants, especially where success has attended a system of economy strained in some respects to an extreme. Yet relying on the good will of those for whom these words are written, I will mention what seem to me to be the immediate or the prospective calls for an increase in the College funds.

First then I will name, although not first in importance, the erection of new buildings. The present ugly row of colleges cannot remain for more than twenty-five years: that is to say one or two of them will probably need to be pulled down within a quarter of a century for very age. It becomes a question whether the system of living in colleges is on the whole the best; or whether as commons have been given up to advantage, so also common halls may not be given up to advantage. I am not sure how the public will decide in this particular. It is certain however that common halls are a gain in point of economy; and the effect which they have of encouraging a common feeling, an esprit du corps, which when well directed is a most healthy and powerful stimulus, ought not wholly to be overlooked; nor has experience shown thus far that there is any gain to College morality from separate residence in private families. Whenever the time shall come for the determination of this question, if new buildings should be found to be desirable, it would then be of the greatest importance to form a new plan, which should give to the College grounds their greatest capacity of embellishment, and which by imposing architecture, should have a healthy effect on the taste and morals of the students. I urge all this, as by no. means to be compared in importance with the intellectual and spiritual advancement of the College: nay I should be alarmed, if the feelings of the graduates under the influence of an imposing magnificent plan of edifices ran in that channel, while higher improvements were necessarily postponed. The College would then be a body adorned and pampered at the cost of the soul. Better even if it raised its intellectual standard, and its buildings lay in ruins.

We pass on then to name what is needed to supply the intellectual wants of the College. Here the state of the material means of instruction may first be noticed. The library although a small is a good one. It consists of not far from 22,000 volumes and has a better fund devoted to its enlargement than is possessed by any other college interest. We do not therefore speak of any great deficiency here. The cabinet likewise is a good one for this country; although quite deficient in the more newly discovered minerals and in the fossil department. The philosophical apparatus is inferior to that of some of the smallest and newly founded colleges, but might be put on a good basis at a small cost. Museums in the departments of natural history are wholly wanting, and will be required, if the contemplated instruction in these branches is to be rendered efficient and useful.

But it is in the means of supporting the proper number of teachers that the College is most deficient. Here the enquiry will first be started, what new branches ought to be introduced? None whatever I reply, but the instruction in some of them ought to be put upon a better basis. Thus provision by permanent funds is needed for instructors in the Romanic, and in the Gothic languages. As these languages, especially French and German, are now taught, they bring a disproportionate separate charge upon term bills; and the small amount received from the students offers no inducement to any man to devote himself to these branches in the exclusive service of the College. There should be two chairs for this kind of instruction, to be filled by Americans who had prepared themselves for their work in Europe. If to this we add that Astronomy may be separated with advantage from Natural Philosophy and form a distinct professorship; and that a chair of history would not be undesirable; we shall have named all the new departments of instruction which seem more particularly to require foundations. And these improvements themselves are not called for before all things else, but may wait their time.

I have already alluded to the inadequate salaries of the existing College officers; and to the fact, that, if any large reduction of students should occur hereafter, even these salaries could not be paid. This appears to me, to be the most pressing among the wants of the College. Hitherto it has been highly respectable to be an officer of Yale College, and men have been willing to renounce more splendid prospects, as far as worldly emolument was concerned, for a connection with one of the oldest and most eminent seats of learning in the country, a connection where they might be both honorably and usefully employed. It has happened too that most of the officers have had other means of support besides their professorships. But this cannot always continue, and meanwhile the expenses and stile of living have been raised here and throughout the country. It will be difficult therefore to find men of the right stamp, who will take places vacated by death or other causes, unless indeed the instruction of the College shall pass out of the hands of Professors into those of an order of Fellows, bound as in the English Universities to reside within the walls of the College buildings, and to remain unmarried. But such a change of officers would probably be highly disastrous; for it would bring instability into instruction and government, and would lower the reputation of the College by committing its entire interests to a younger and less permanent set of men. In view of all this the friends of the College are urgently called upon to consider the importance of enlarging that part of its permanent funds which is not specifically appropriated, that it may meet any calls of the kind already mentioned, or such other important ones, as may be made from time to time.

There is another kind of benefactions to which I wish to call attention. They are the endowment of scholarships and fellowships. We have already five undergraduate scholarships, all of them created within the last four years, and filled on examination according to merit. They have been attended with the happiest results; but are too few to produce competition, except within a small circle of students. The existing ones have a fund, four of them of a thousand dollars each, and one of about fourteen hundred dollars.

Graduate scholarships appear to me to be still more important, both directly as enabling young men to pursue particular branches of study, for which they have a turn after their graduation; and indirectly, as raising the tone of scholarship through their means, and as fitting them for a literary and professional life. Of such scholarships there are five at Yale College, viz.: three on Bishop Berkeley's foundation, and two on Mr. Sheldon Clark's: but they fail of acting as a great incitement as well on account of the small amount of the fund,—Mr. Clark's yielding one hundred and twenty dollars to each scholar, and Berkeley's about forty-five,—as from the fact that they can be held only two and three years. I am persuaded that scholarships for graduates, properly guarded by provisions requiring a certain amount or a certain kind of study, giving a support, even though a small one, to the incumbent, and capable of being retained for five or ten years, would have the happiest bearing upon the standard of scholarship; and if the plan were adopted generally, upon the general cultivation of the country.

www.ingramcontent.com/pod-product-compliance
Lightning Source LLC
LaVergne TN
LVHW021417110826
845150LV00007B/1958

9781425509705